BOULDER

BOULDER

EVOLUTION OF A CITY

REVISED EDITION

SILVIA PETTEM

WITH A FOREWORD BY
LISTON E. LEYENDECKER

UNIVERSITY PRESS OF COLORADO

To Boulder's early photographers

Published by the University Press of Colorado
5589 Arapahoe Avenue, Suite 206C
Boulder, Colorado 80303

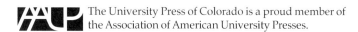 The University Press of Colorado is a proud member of
the Association of American University Presses.

The University Press of Colorado is a cooperative publishing enterprise supported, in part,
by Adams State College, Colorado State University, Fort Lewis College, Mesa State College,
Metropolitan State College of Denver, University of Colorado, University of Northern
Colorado, and Western State College of Colorado.

∞ The paper used in this publication meets the minimum requirements of the American
National Standard for Information Sciences—Permanence of Paper for Printed Library
Materials. ANSI Z39.48-1992

Library of Congress Cataloging-in-Publication Data

Pettem, Silvia.
  Boulder : evolution of a city / Silvia Pettem.— Rev. ed.
      p. cm.
  Includes bibliographical references and index.
  ISBN-13: 978-0-87081-831-8 (pbk. : alk. paper)
  ISBN-10: 0-87081-831-7 (pbk. : alk. paper) 1. Boulder (Colo.)—History—Pictorial works.
I. Title.
  F784.B66P48 2006
  978.8'63—dc22
                                        2006003433

Design by Daniel Pratt

15   14   13   12   11   10   09   08   07   06   10   9   8   7   6   5   4   3   2   1

CONTENTS

FOREWORD

Boulder received its start in the late fall of 1858 when gold rush participants erected log cabins for shelter just below the mouth of Boulder Canyon. In January 1859, these newcomers ventured 12 miles farther west and 3,000 feet higher up to locate the mining camp of Gold Hill. Their tiny settlement at the canyon's entrance served as a supply point for people entering and leaving the newly found gold region. Thus, Boulder's population came to consist of businessmen, entrepreneurs, and their families, rather than the transient, unstable, rough-and-tumble elements of the mining camps. Although the community did possess its fair share of hard cases, prostitutes, and saloonkeepers, these particular groups were not destined to remain.

High prices for scarce agricultural produce led dwellers to plant gardens in 1859. Residents also formed a town company, while they platted and mapped the site, so that at the end of 1859 the former camp boasted some seventy cabins. The following year, a frame house, a wooden commercial structure filled with goods, and a school graced the town. Boulderites also took steps, even before the first Colorado Territorial legislature convened in 1861, to ensure that their community would house the University of Colorado.

After the first mining excitement to the west subsided, Boulder's survival became a struggle, but the town did not fade from the mainstream of Colorado history. Instead, it served as county seat while catering to the needs of neighboring farmers and coal miners and—once the university began holding classes—those of the state. The town incorporated in November 1871, as people moved to it from other parts of the Colorado Territory. Soon to follow was the arrival of railroads in 1873. By 1890, Boulder's population stood at close to four thousand souls.

An early twentieth-century oil boom did not materialize into permanent production, but Boulder survived, becoming more of a cultural center as it weathered Prohibition and the Great Depression. By the end of World War II, its chief support lay with the university and smokeless industry.

In the chapters that follow, Silvia Pettem employs Boulder's architecture to portray its social history; she uses contemporary photographs of street scenes and individual buildings to illustrate the development of separate sections of the town. She supplements early pictures of a neighborhood or building with a recent photograph of the same vicinity or structure. Her readers should not experience difficulty finding an old edifice or, if it no longer stands, locating its site.

Local historians will find a great deal of good information between the end boards of this very useful chronicle. Longtime area residents will find plenty of material to chew on as they reminisce about scenes and places covered in these pages. Newcomers will enjoy the opportunity to see how Boulder looked before their arrival, and nonresidents will be able to learn how this community has evolved into one of the state's most sophisticated cities.

LISTON E. LEYENDECKER, 1994
PROFESSOR OF HISTORY,
COLORADO STATE UNIVERSITY

PREFACE

arious locations in Boulder are shown in two, three, or sometimes four different time periods. It's tempting to refer to these views as "then and now" photographs, but history is a continuum and is always changing. This process is evident in some of the recent photographs, which are already outdated. Note what has changed, but, more important, look for what has been preserved. I hope that the reader of this book, whether for enjoyment or reference, will find something new in Boulder's past, will come to appreciate how the city has evolved, and will be able to apply this knowledge toward Boulder's future.

In visualizing locations of streets and buildings, remember:

+ Mountains are to the west.

+ Address numbers on the north and west sides of the streets are odd.

+ Address numbers on the south and east sides of the streets are even.

+ Address numbers on the east and west streets get larger from west to east.

+ Address numbers on the north and south streets get larger from south to north.

As much as possible, I researched information from primary sources, including maps, city directories, and photographs. I also consulted original newspaper accounts and historical documents. I have only two regrets: that trees often prevented me from taking the current photos from the exact locations as in the older photos and that it was impossible to include everyone's favorite location.

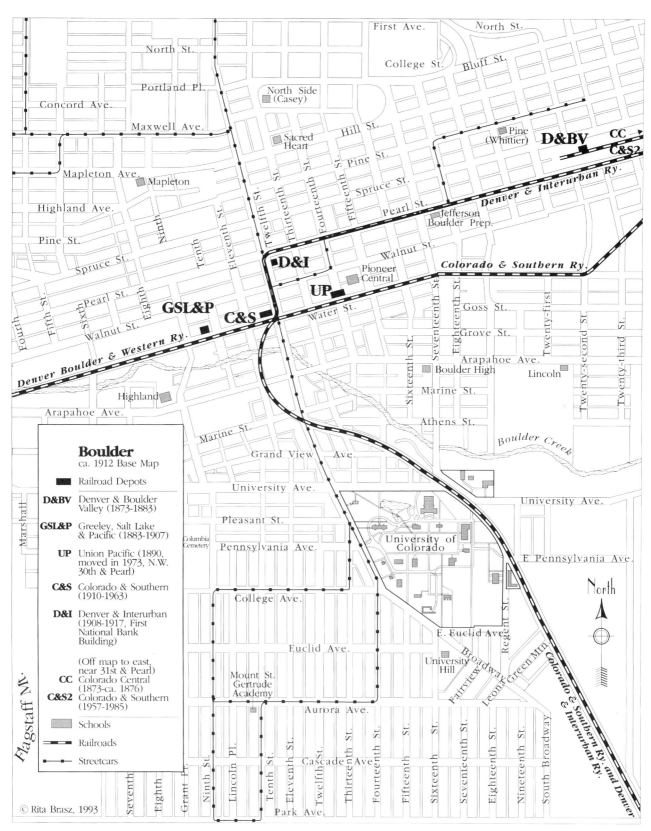

Boulder's schools and railroad depots (identified by the railroads that built them) are plotted on a base map, ca. 1912. The section of Boulder shown extends from Park Avenue (Baseline Road) north to First (Alpine) Avenue.

ACKNOWLEDGMENTS

Many people were involved in this book's first edition, published in 1994. Of everyone previously acknowledged, I particularly wish to thank, once again, former Carnegie Branch Library for Local History manager Lois Anderton. In the intervening years, Carnegie Library's current team (Wendy Hall, Mary Jo Reitsema, and Marti Anderson) has continued Lois's commitment to excellence in helping and guiding all researchers of Boulder history. I'm also very grateful for the encouragement and support of *Daily Camera* librarian Carol Taylor. My thanks, too, go to Gail Hellerling and Jesse Newcomb, who arranged for me to climb to the roof of the Boulder County Courthouse to take the cover photograph.

BOULDER

CHAPTER ONE

EARLY BOULDER PHOTOGRAPHERS

arly-day photographers didn't have an easy time. Exclusive of darkroom supplies, they carried around a big camera, a heavy wooden tripod, and a box of glass plates. Their outfit weighed about 75 pounds. The excellent record we have of Boulder today is due to the skill and perseverance of Boulder's early photographers.

Before the advent of photographic film, photographs were exposed on 5" x 7", 8" x 10", or even larger plates of glass. The larger the plate, the larger the picture, as photographs generally weren't enlarged during processing. Boulder's earliest photographers used "wet" plates, a process developed ca. 1851 to replace the earlier daguerreotypes. Ether, alcohol, and chemicals were floated in collodion on a glass plate. As soon as the ether or alcohol evaporated, but while the plate was still wet, the photographer dipped the plate in a solution of silver nitrate, then put the glass plate in the camera and took a photograph. It had to be developed at

once. If the photographer was away from his or her studio, a portable darkroom in a wagon or tent was required.

By 1880, cameras still were large and heavy, but the advent of the "dry plate" process made photography easier by eliminating the necessity of preparing fresh emulsion for each photograph. Commercial dry glass negatives were presensitized and precoated with a light-sensitive silver bromide. They could be stored until needed and printed later. Glass plates of this type were used by professional photographers through the late 1920s.

In the early days, albumen-coated paper was printed directly by passing sunlight through the glass plate and onto the paper. The paper was toned through submersion in a bath of gold chloride; then the photograph was fixed, air-dried, and glued onto cardboard with wheat paste.

One of Boulder's earliest resident photographers was Robert L. Thompson. As early as 1869, he advertised in the *Boulder County Pioneer*. His studio and residence were on the southwest corner of 12th (Broadway) and Spruce Streets. The house was moved when the Willard Block replaced it in 1898, the year Thompson died. He also was the choir director of the First Congregational Church, where his brother, Reverend Nathan Thompson, was minister. In 1872, while continuing with his photographic business, Robert Thompson became the official territorial assayer for Colorado.

Alexander Martin went into partnership with Thompson in 1873. Later he had a photographic gallery of his own. Martin remained in business in Boulder until 1878.

Numerous other photographers were active in the 1870s and 1880s. Richard B. Collins and J. Henfield showed up in 1876. Mrs. L. A. McGreagor had a photographic studio in 1878. Mr. Gregg had one in 1879.

Photographers in the 1880s included Joseph E. Streeter, Frederick Law, Isaac H. Hosier, Ben Sooy, King & Company, D. B. Yale, and Charles Weitfle, who in 1882 photographed the laying of the original Boulder County Court House cornerstone.

Others followed in the 1890s. Photographers included E. E. McGraw, L. Moore, Burns and Company, Mary Dudley, D. G. Clark, S. J. Clark, A. T. Wheeler, Lloyd E. Nelson, W. F. Freeman, and the Black sisters, A. E. Black and Minnie C. Black.

JOSEPH BEVIER STURTEVANT ("ROCKY MOUNTAIN JOE")

Early Boulder's most prolific photographer, Joseph Bevier Sturtevant, arrived in Boulder from Wisconsin in 1876 at age twenty-five. He thought of himself first as an artist, sketching buildings and mountain views. To earn a living, he painted houses, signs, and theater scenery, and hung wallpaper.

One itinerant lecturer commissioned him to paint the Seven Hills of Rome.

In 1884, he turned his talent to photography. By 1886, the *Boulder County Herald* was editorializing on Sturtevant's newly acquired skill by reporting that he spent July 4 of that year photographing "baseballers" in the mountain town of Sunshine.

Sturtevant had several studio locations. In 1893 and 1894 (see Chapter 9 for details of the Chatauqua

This studio portrait shows Joseph Bevier Sturtevant in his usual Rocky Mountain Joe image, complete with buckskin clothing, long hair, mustache, goatee, and camera. *Carnegie Branch Library for Local History, Boulder Historical Society Collection.*

movement), he was in partnership with Louis Meile. When Chautauqua opened in 1898, Sturtevant was on the scene with his photographic studio, called "Rocky Mountain Joe's Place—The Woodbine." He was considered "a colorful character," with long hair, mustache, goatee, and the clothes of an Indian scout, which he claimed to have been.

"Rocky Mountain Joe," as he was called, had a way with women. For instance, when driving a stagecoach with tourists in the mountains, and being told that one of the young women's names was "Mary," Sturtevant would point with a flourish to a mountain and say, "There is Mount Mary."

His wife, Anna, and their children, helped him with the business. They sold cabinet-sized photographs, 3⅞" x 5½" mounted on a card, of Boulder scenes for 10¢ each. Other photographers complained about being undercut. At least two of his galleries were named "The Cabinet" because of his specialty.

After his wife died, Sturtevant took to the bottle and was briefly married again. He started, but never finished, an illustrated book of poetry titled *Sparkling Gems of the Rocky Mountains*. His topics ranged from humorous to sentimental, always displaying deep affection for Boulder. In his dedication, he wrote, "Please do not criticize me too strongly, should all not run smoothly, for little breaks oftimes show up one's life."

Sturtevant was found dead in 1910, lying along the railroad tracks between Denver and Boulder. Speculation was that he hadn't had fare for the Interurban Railroad and had probably fallen trying to get on a moving train.

Martin R. Parsons, pioneer stagecoach driver and personal friend, salvaged and preserved thirty-five hundred glass plates from Sturtevant's home after his death. Parson's initials, "MRP," appear on all of the plates that he found. However, not all of the glass negatives in Sturtevant's possession had been his own photographs, so MRP is not enough to identify a photograph as being taken by Sturtevant.

Sturtevant and Parsons are buried in Columbia Cemetery.

LOUIS MEILE

After being in partnership with Sturtevant, Louis Meile started a studio of his own. His specialty was portraits and commercial photography, but he's known for his photographs of the "100-year flood" in 1894. It was said that at the height of the flood, Sturtevant was stranded on the south side of Boulder Creek, with his camera and equipment on the north side.

Meile moved with his family to Haxtun, in northeastern Colorado, where he homesteaded a farm. Later, they returned to Boulder, where Meile died in 1935 at the age of seventy-seven. Like Sturtevant, Meile is buried in Columbia Cemetery.

LAWRENCE P. BASS

In 1888, Lawrence P. Bass was in partnership with Isaac H. Hosier. By 1892, Bass had his own studio. Although he continued as a commercial photographer, Bass also was a Boulder policeman from 1896 to 1920. He died when his police car was hit by a speeding fire truck.

Photographers of the early 1900s included Charles E. Gosha, C. A. Wales, George F. Britton, H. L. York, Pearl C. Lux, Flo E. Satterfield, William Hassebroeck, and Thomas C. Black (no relation to the earlier Black sisters). Thomas C. Black came

Lawrence P. Bass was both a commercial photographer and a Boulder policeman. *Carnegie Branch Library for Local History, Boulder Historical Society Daily Camera Collection.*

J. RAYMOND BRACKETT

J. Raymond Brackett came from Maine to Boulder in 1884 to teach English, Greek, and comparative literature at the University of Colorado. He was the first dean of the College of Liberal Arts (in 1892) as well as the first Dean of the Graduate School (in 1909).

His 6" x 8" glass plate negatives of university scenes spanned the years 1890–1915. Thirty-six of his university photos were on display at the Columbian Exhibition in Chicago in 1893, commemorating (one year late) the 400th anniversary of Christopher Columbus's landing in America. Brackett traveled extensively, and, when back in Boulder, displayed his photographs of England, Italy, Greece, and Japan.

Brackett died in 1922 at the age of sixty-eight and is buried in Columbia Cemetery.

ED TANGEN

Ed Tangen came to the United States from his native Norway as a child and moved to Boulder from Chicago in 1900. He was a bachelor who enjoyed hiking in the mountains and was active with the Rocky Mountain Climbers' Club. For half a century, his studio remained on the second floor of the Ehrlich Block, on 14th Street across from the Boulder County Court House. He was on the scene of whatever was going on downtown.

Many of his photographs were stereographs. He used a special stereographic camera with two lenses mounted about three inches apart. They produced two images on one glass plate. As the photographs were from slightly different angles, they gave perspective to the scene when viewed through a stereopticon. The viewer, invented by doctor/poet Oliver Wendell Holmes, was common around the turn of the twentieth century.

from Alabama and worked as an engineer on the Colorado & Northwestern Railroad before becoming a commercial photographer. Many of his photographs were published in the *Daily Camera.*

Although Sturtevant and other late nineteenth-century professional photographers continued to use dry glass plates, by the late 1880s, George Eastman, of Rochester, New York, had developed an amateur camera he named the "Kodak." It used a paper film instead of glass, and was the forerunner of photography as we know it today.

Ed Tangen, "The Pictureman," took many Boulder scenes as well as this self-portrait. *Carnegie Branch Library for Local History, Boulder Historical Society Daily Camera Collection.*

tion. He stated, "In this world of lies, deception, and hypocrisy, an ounce of honest circumstantial evidence is worth pounds of oral testimony." A Wyoming woman guilty of murdering her husband thought she would go free. When she found out that Tangen was going to testify against her, she hanged herself. From 1923, to 1951, when he died, Tangen was the offical "identification officer" for the Boulder County Sheriff's Office and was in demand in the courtrooms of several western states.

CHARLES F. SNOW

Charles F. Snow bought Charles F. Gosha's studio at 2028 14th Street, near the Curran Theatre, in 1908. His partner was Georgie McNaught. Two years

Georgie and Charles Snow worked together in the Snow Photography Studio for forty years. *Author's collection.*

Tangen continued to use glass plates into the 1920s and took a variety of scenes, including panoramas, in and around Boulder. Many are signed with his trademark, a "T" in a diamond.

Photography was also part of Tangen's long career in criminal investigation. His microphotographs were a revolutionary method for linking a specific bullet to a specific gun, thus providing evidence in the courtroom. He compiled and photographed an extensive collection of bullets. He then cataloged and cross-indexed them as to type of rifling, make of gun, and caliber of ammuni-

later, they were married, and they jointly ran the business until her death in 1948. In the later years, the studio was located at 1909 Broadway.

With Edith Pendleton, his second wife, Snow continued to take portraits, his specialty. He believed in capturing natural expressions and catching his subjects off guard. Snow was also known for his landscapes and photographs of the University of Colorado. He was made a fellow of the Royal Photographic Society in England and was president of the American Society of Photographers.

EBEN G. FINE

Eben G. Fine was a pharmacist at Temple Drug Store in the Masonic Temple Building. He was a friend of Ed Tangen, whose studio was just across the intersection. For Fine, photography began as a hobby. Then Fine began giving illustrated lectures, and soon he was in demand all over the country, particularly in the Midwest and South. He was hired by the Burlington Railroad, and endorsed by the Boulder Chamber of Commerce, to give two-month lecture tours each spring to publicize and encourage people to come to Colorado. His glass lantern slides were pictures of his own photographs, which were then colored and projected on a screen.

Fine was very active in civic affairs. Eben G. Fine Park, between Arapahoe Avenue and Canyon Boulevard near the mouth of Boulder Canyon, was named for him.

CHAPTER TWO

DOWNTOWN BUSINESS DISTRICT
THE PEARL STREET MALL

A. Brookfield, one of Boulder's first prospectors, wrote in a letter to his wife, "We thought that as the weather would not permit us to mine, we would lay out and commence to build what may be an important town." On February 10, 1859, shortly after gold was discovered near present-day Gold Hill, fifty-four men formed the Boulder City Town Company and platted 100 lots.

According to a 1903 written interview with George R. Williamson, another early prospector, a stick was driven into the middle of the present intersection of Broadway and Pearl Streets. Then, to determine a straight line for Pearl Street, "a sighting [was made] across this stick to the black spur in the prairie, known as Valmont Butte." Recent surveys have shown, however, that Walnut (then Front) Street, which parallels Pearl Street, is directly in line with the highest point of the butte.

Colorado, and even Colorado Territory, didn't exist in 1859. The Kansas-Nebraska Act of 1854 had placed "Boulder City" in Nebraska Territory, which belonged to the Indians. But the prospectors stayed anyway. In 1855, Congress had passed the Bounty Law, which gave veterans of the Revolutionary War and/or their widows 160 acres of public land in "the West." The following year, Maine resident Sarah Weston, the ninety-three-year-old widow of veteran Joseph Weston, applied for and received Land Warrant 36557.

It's not clear what happened next, but land grants were transferable. It is believed that a member of the Parlin or Bixby families, both neighbors in Maine who moved to Boulder, may have purchased the land grant. At some point, it was sold or transferred to Judge Peter M. Housel, who later received a patent from the U. S. government for the southwest quarter of section 30, which became downtown Boulder.

The town, consisting of a few log cabins, was centered around 12th (Broadway) and Pearl Streets. Except for a few cottonwoods, willows, and box elders along Boulder Creek, there were no trees. Isabella Bird, an adventurous Englishwoman who traveled through Boulder on horseback a few years later, called Boulder "a hideous collection of frame houses on the burning plain."

Gold miners in Gold Hill and Ward were dependent on Boulder for their supplies. Boulder grew steadily following the 1869 discovery of silver at Caribou and gold-bearing telluride ores at Gold Hill in 1872. Brick and stone commercial buildings began to replace the frame businesses on Pearl Street. (A building was called a "block" if it contained two or more storefronts.) Street merchants delighted Pearl Street crowds with flaring gaslights and displays of ventriloquism in order to sell hair restoratives, electric belts for rheumatism, and other cure-alls.

Boulder, with mining and agriculture as its base, became a sophisticated city in the early 1900s. The business district, comprising late nineteenth- and early twentieth-century buildings, was nestled between the new residential areas on Mapleton Hill and University Hill. Hardwoods and fruit trees were imported from the East. Perhaps to ensure tree planting, downtown streets included those named Spruce and Pine. In 1890, Front Street was renamed Walnut Street.

To obtain the best drinking water, the city purchased the watershed of the Arapaho Glacier and later the glacier itself. A $200,000 steel pipeline brought the 99.996 percent pure water all the way from an intake pipe on Boulder County Ranch, now Caribou Ranch, to the Chautauqua and Sunshine Reservoirs in Boulder. All over Boulder, drinking fountains were installed that read "Pure Cold Water from the Boulder-Owned Arapahoe [sic] Glacier." The only drinking fountain still marked today is in the Hotel Boulderado.

By the early twentieth century, shoppers could buy just about anything they wanted in Boulder. For women, there were imported perfumes, diamond lockets, plumed hats, button shoes, and even rust-proof corsets. Both dress goods and ready-to-wear clothing were available.

Stores stocked gourmet foods such as oysters, a selection of coffee, and choice and smoked meats. The Seventh Day Adventist Church, operators of the Boulder Colorado Sanitarium, manufactured its own line of whole-grain cereals and health foods.

During Thanksgiving week 1909, Boulder celebrated the fiftieth anniversary (semicentennial) of the settlement of Boulder County. Pharmacist and photographer Eben G. Fine arranged for a band of Utes to come from southern Colorado to join in the festivities. He succeeded in getting "Buckskin Charlie" and his friends to take part in a staged holdup on what is now Boulder High School's athletic field. "Johnny" Carmack raced down 17th Street in his Concord stagecoach. The Utes rushed out of a thicket and tried to overtake the coach, while cowboys came out shooting, rescued the passengers, and drove the Utes away. Everyone thought the holdup was fun.

Other activities included a large parade and a demonstration by the fire department. In the Armory Building on Pearl Street, five hundred people sat down to a banquet honoring Boulder's pioneers. The "Queen" was "Auntie" Brookfield, the recipient of the letter from her prospector-husband half a century before. Around her were all of the surviving accredited "fifty-niners" and twenty-two maids of honor representing each Boulder County community.

Meanwhile, university students paraded up and down Pearl Street with red and green torches.

They then held a "monster" bonfire pep rally, complete with Ute dances, prior to their football game the next day against the Colorado School of Mines.

Streetcars were an efficient means of public transportation within the city. Boys on bicycles darted around a new invention—the automobile. In 1909, it was still a novelty, but people were taking notice. A newspaper reporter wrote, "Three young bloods stirred all Boulder by careening all over town at a reckless speed in an auto."

The Denver & Interurban's electrically powered trains made sixteen round-trips per day between Boulder and Denver. From 1908 to 1917, this cheap, clean, and efficient means of public transportation ran down Pearl Street on its way to Louisville, Broomfield, and Denver. Between 1917 and 1926, the Interurbans stopped at the Union Pacific depot and alternated their routes with runs through the university and Marshall. Either way, businessmen arrived at their destinations relaxed, walked to their appointments, and, when finished, got back on the trains.

Railroads to Brighton, Denver, and Cheyenne connected with points east and west. Narrow-gauge railroads served the mountain towns. Soon, automobiles began to replace stagecoaches, and trucks, instead of wagons, carried freight.

In the 1930s, people didn't seem interested in their architectural past. Storefronts were lowered and modernized. When the inside of Boulder's original court house burned, the building was torn down and replaced with a new one. People were caught up in parades for the Fourth of July, Pow Wow, and Armistice Day. They all went down Pearl Street.

During wartime, few changes were made in Boulder. One exception was the renaming of the section of 12th Street that ran through downtown. It became Broadway.

Post–World War II growth and the increasing popularity of the automobile took businesses away from downtown. Metal siding covered up what was left. Parking was not a problem. The North Broadway, Arapahoe Village, and Basemar Shopping Centers were built in the 1950s.

In 1963, when the first segment of Crossroads Shopping Center was built, Boulder merchants and property owners organized "Boulder Tomorrow, Inc." to help plan the redevelopment of the downtown area. Construction of a downtown pedestrian mall began in 1976 and was completed in 1977. The mall eliminated traffic on Pearl Street between 11th and 15th Streets. Attitudes changed with the times, and historic preservation came into style. Businesses as well as street merchants, returned downtown. Many of Boulder's original buildings were restored.

After the Denver & Interurban was discontinued in 1926, electrically powered trains were replaced by the buses of the Denver & Interurban Motor Company. They, in turn, were succeeded by the buses of the Denver Boulder Bus Company, taken over by the Regional Transportation District (RTD) in 1974. The Denver Boulder Bus Company used the Union Pacific depot. Later, RTD buses stopped at the former Arnold Brothers Ford Building, on the northwest corner of 9th Street and Canyon Boulevard, until the RTD Transit Center was built on 14th Street next to the former location of the Union Pacific depot.

History repeats itself. With the downtown business district revitalized, planners are again talking about new forms of public transportation.

Boulder's early architecture was similar to that of other Western towns, with flat false fronts on frame buildings, uneven board sidewalks, and dirt streets. Louis Garbarino's Saloon, at 1106 Pearl, was wedged between the brick Bush and Ellet Block (housing A. W. Bush and Company jewelers and John A. Ellet's real estate office) and People's Meat Market on the southeast corner of 11th and Pearl Streets. *Photo by Alexander Martin, ca. 1875. Carnegie Branch Library for Local History, Boulder Historical Society Collection.*

The Bush and Ellet Block is to the left of Old Chicago Restaurant and Bar, which is on the site of Garbarino's Saloon. Old Chicago is in the Garbarino Garage Building, which replaced Garbarino's Saloon and the People's Meat Market. The garage was operated by Louis Garbarino's son, Belshe Garbarino, from ca. 1917 through the late 1920s. *Photo by author, 2005.*

Louis Garbarino's Saloon was one of a dozen on Pearl Street. In the late 1880s, it was considered so disreputable that Boulder citizens insisted on removing all tables and chairs to prevent loafing. Garbarino fought back by selling "two Schooners for a nickel," complete with a free lunch. The saloon remained in business until ca. 1903. A year or two later, Louis Garbarino died. Photo ca. 1880s–1890s. *Carnegie Branch Library for Local History, Boulder Historical Society Collection.*

Old Chicago Bar is on the site of Garbarino's Saloon. *Photo by Brad Niederman, 1993. Carnegie Branch Library for Local History, Boulder Historical Society Collection.*

The Cheney Block, completed in 1899, replaced Boulder's first hotel, the Boulder House, on the northeast corner of 11th and Pearl Streets. It was renamed the Buckingham Block in 1905. Offices and a meeting room for secret societies were upstairs. Retailers were in the storefronts below. When this photo was taken, the Lucky Inn served 3.2 percent beer, all that was permitted in Boulder between 1933 and 1967. National Prohibition had been repealed, but Boulder had voted itself "dry" in 1907 and couldn't sell liquor for the next sixty years. Photo 1941. *Carnegie Branch Library for Local History, Boulder Historical Society Daily Camera Collection.*

Today, the Boulder Bookstore occupies much of this building, including the impressive meeting room with stained glass windows on the second floor above 11th Street. Entrances to the bookstore are from both 11th and Pearl Streets. Other retail stores fill the corner storefronts. *Photo by author, 2005.*

This view of the north side of Pearl Street, between 11th Street and Broadway, shows the Buckingham Block on the left. In the foreground is the Boulder High School Marching Band. Photo ca. 1942. *Carnegie Branch Library for Local History, Boulder Historical Society Daily Camera Collection.*

The Bookend Café is under the arched windows, now partially obscured by trees. *Photo by author, 2005.*

Charles Boettcher was a hardware merchant who built the Boettcher Building in 1878, then sold his business to his cousin and followed the silver mining boom to Leadville. His store was on the southwest corner of 12th (Broadway) and Pearl Streets, ahead and to the left of the cow. George F. Fonda was already in business in the white building on the left, which said "Drug Store." *Photo by Joseph Bevier Sturtevant, 1885. Carnegie Branch Library for Local History, Boulder Historical Society Collection.*

Boulder got 3 feet in two days during the "big snow" of December 4 and 5, 1913. In this view looking west from the intersection of 12th (Broadway) and Pearl Streets, the Boettcher Building is on the left. J. W. Valentine had established the Valentine Hardware Company there in 1907. Boulder Business College was upstairs. Photo 1913. *Carnegie Branch Library for Local History, Boulder Historical Society Daily Camera Collection.*

When this photo was taken from the same intersection, John B. Valentine had joined his father in the Valentine Hardware Company, and the Metropolitan Hotel was upstairs. The secretary of the Chamber of Commerce, Francis Reich, painted "Interesting Facts About Boulder" and a large map of Boulder County on the east side of the building. The First National Bank was across 12th Street. Photo 1938. *Carnegie Branch Library for Local History, Boulder Historical Society Collection.*

The Valentine Hardware Company remained in business for sixty-three years. Today the Boettcher Building contains other retail businesses. The large painted map on the side of the building disappeared in the 1950s. The Pearl Street pedestrian mall, completed in 1977, removed traffic from Pearl Street between 11th and 15th Streets. *Photo by author, 2005.*

The first building of the First National Bank was built in 1877 on the southeast corner of 12th (Broadway) and Pearl Streets. It was replaced in 1881 with the second First National Bank building, shown here on the right. *Photo by Lawrence P. Bass, 1893. Carnegie Branch Library for Local History, Boulder Historical Society Collection.*

In 1956, the Mercantile Bank and Trust Company moved to the site of the Monticello Hotel on the southeast corner of Walnut and 13th Streets. The First National Bank (which became Bank One) moved in 1958 to the northeast corner of Water Street (Canyon Boulevard) and Broadway. *Photo by author, 2005.*

This panorama, looking east on Pearl Street from 12th Street (Broadway), was taken just after the completion of the third building of the First National Bank on the right. Offices were upstairs. Half (the width of three windows) of the previous bank building remained. All three First National Bank buildings up to this date were on the same site. The second building of the Mercantile Bank, on the left, was built in 1912. In 1917, this section of Pearl, between 12th (Broadway) and 15th Streets, was the first street in Boulder to be paved. *Photo by Ed Tangen, 1921. Carnegie Branch Library for Local History, Boulder Historical Society Collection.*

Boulder's first brick commercial building, owned by Charles Dabney and Andrew J. Macky, is clearly shown in this earliest known photo of Pearl Street. After a major fire in 1883, the west side of the building, owned by Dabney, was repaired. The east side, which Macky owned, was torn down. In 1884, Macky replaced his side with a larger brick building, which is still standing. In the foreground on the northwest corner of Pearl and 13th Streets was the Colorado House, a hotel built in 1863. It was torn down in 1881 and replaced with the first building of the National State Bank, of which the east half was later remodeled for the Boulder National Bank. Photo 1866. *Carnegie Branch Library for Local History, Boulder Historical Society Collection.*

Art Source International is in the building formerly occupied by the Public Drug Company. The Peppercorn is to the left in the building that was originally Bradley and McClure Dry Goods. It later became the White-Davis Mercantile Company, and from 1936 to 1986 was the Brooks Fauber Dry Goods Company. *Photo by author, 2005.*

Company B troops were leaving for World War I in this view of the north side of Pearl Street. Visible to the right of the Mercantile Bank is the newer Macky Block, which replaced the east side of the original Dabney-Macky Building. The Rogers Block was embellished with two bay windows and roofline ornaments. The next bay window was in a narrow separate building. The next building was the White-Davis Mercantile Company, followed by Public Drug Company, the People's Store, and the Boulder National Bank. First-floor businesses had high ceilings, high storefronts, and large awnings. *Photo by Out West studio, 1917. Carnegie Branch Library for Local History, Boulder Historical Society Collection.*

This close-up of Dabney's half of the first brick building in Boulder was on the northeast corner of 12th (Broadway) and Pearl Streets. To the east was Macky's new building. In 1899, Dabney's building was torn down and replaced with another brick building. Then that building was replaced with the Mercantile Bank. The Rogers Block, on the right, had bay windows. Photo ca. 1898. *Carnegie Branch Library for Local History, Boulder Historical Society Collection.*

Shortly after completion in 1912, the second building of the Mercantile Bank dominated the northeast corner of 12th (Broadway) and Pearl Streets. The first building of the Mercantile Bank was at 2027 12th (Broadway), built in 1904 on the site of Ben Williams's blacksmith shop. The bank contained a room for its customers for "correspondence, resting, and to meet friends downtown." *Carnegie Branch Library for Local History, Boulder Historical Society Collection.*

In 1937, the Rogers Block was "modernized" by having its bay windows and pointed roofline ornamentation removed and the storefront lowered. Smith Shoe Company moved in from across the street. The Colorado Hotel, on the second floor, began as a rooming house in 1908 and operated until 1975. Crowder's covered half of the Macky Building, and the building next to it, with metal siding. *Photo by John B. Schoolland, 1966. Carnegie Branch Library for Local History, Boulder, John B. Schoolland Collection.*

Square windows give a feel of the old bay windows that were once a part of the Rogers Block. New retail stores replace Smith Shoe Company, operated by the Smith family and in the same location for decades. *Photo by author, 2005.*

The Frank Jordinelli's Saloon and Liquor Store Building, at 1230 Pearl Street, was very similar to the George F. Fonda Building a few doors to the west at 1218 Pearl. The same ornate cast-iron façade, purchased by mail order, was repeated again at 1410 Pearl, former home of Rocky Mountain Joe's Café, named for photographer Joseph Bevier Sturtevant. *Photo by Joseph Bevier Sturtevant, ca. 1898–1906. Carnegie Branch Library for Local History, Boulder Historical Society Collection.*

In the 1950s, it was fashionable to cover up historic buildings with painted corrugated metal siding. Jones Drugs was in the adulterated Jordinelli Building from 1955 to 1962. Glens Camera was its tenant from 1963 to 1975. Next door was the Charcoal Chef restaurant. *Photo by John B. Schoolland, 1966. Carnegie Branch Library for Local History, Boulder, John B. Schoolland Collection.*

Glens Camera and the Charcoal Chef vacated their buildings prior to the pedestrian mall construction. The downtown business district had deteriorated, and parking was not a problem. Photo 1976. *Carnegie Branch Library for Local History, Boulder, Downtown Boulder Mall Collection.*

The Jordinelli Building and the ones to the left were razed in 1976 for future expansion of the National State Bank. The building to the right, now occupied by Art Mart (note the same arched windows), hasn't changed. *Photo by author, 2005.*

The Brookfield-Holstein Block was built in 1881 on the site of an early hotel, the Colorado House, on the northwest corner of 13th and Pearl Streets. The east half was the National State Bank until 1896, when that bank moved out (temporarily into the Masonic Temple Building) and Boulder National Bank moved in. Photo ca. 1890. *Carnegie Branch Library for Local History, Boulder, John B. Schoolland Collection.*

In 1899, the Boulder National Bank section of the building was extensively remodeled. When this photo was taken, the bank still had its name on the building, a year after closing in the Great Depression. The popcorn wagon, with a gasoline-fueled steam engine, was operated by George T. Johnson and his son, Chester A. Johnson, at this intersection from 1916 to 1956. *Photo by Ed Tangen, 1934. Carnegie Branch Library for Local History, Boulder Historical Society Collection.*

Like other downtown buildings, the Boulder National Bank Building was covered up and "modernized" in the 1950s. Majestic Savings occupied this location from the late 1960s to the early 1980s. Photo 1976. *Carnegie Branch Library for Local History, Boulder, Communication Arts Collection.*

The siding is now removed, and the turret-like bay window over the entrance is revealed. Note the extension of the cornice and roofline to include the rest of the original building to the left. *Photo by author, 2005.*

A temporary welcome arch at the intersection of 13th and Pearl Streets was erected for a convention of the Knights of Pythias. Streamer's Drug Store, on the southwest corner, was replaced with the National State Bank Building. At the time, the National State Bank was on the northwest corner of the intersection. In 1899, that building was extensively remodeled by the Boulder National Bank. An iceman's wagon is under the arch. Court House Square is to the right. *Photo by Joseph Bevier Sturtevant, 1895. Carnegie Branch Library for Local History, Boulder Historical Society Collection.*

National State Bank had moved into the new Masonic Temple Building in 1896 after being located in the Brookfield-Holstein Block. The bank opened its new building, on the southwest corner of 13th and Pearl Streets, on New Year's Day, 1900. A *Daily Camera* reporter described the upstairs offices as "quite a lawyers' roost." The National State Bank clock was put up in 1919. *Photo by Charles F. Snow, 1925. Carnegie Branch Library for Local History, Boulder Historical Society Collection.*

The National State Bank's interior was elaborately decorated and even included a display case of Boulder County mineral specimens. On the left was director and vice president James C. Hankins. In the booth were cashier J. H. Nicholson and assistant cashier William S. Bellman. Photo ca. 1900. *Carnegie Branch Library for Local History, Boulder Historical Society Collection.*

In 1955, National State Bank expanded into the western part of the building previously occupied by Jones Drug Store. In 1976, the four buildings to the west (with tenants Tarzan's Place, Colorado Barber Shop, Tylers Restaurant, and Glens Camera) were torn down for future bank expansion. The clock was moved to a pedestal on the mall. The roof ornamentation on the bank has been removed, as have the words "state bank." Now this is Wells Fargo Bank. *Photo by author, 2005.*

This photo, looking west from the intersection of 13th and Pearl Streets, was on the front page of the *Daily Camera's Industrial Supplement* in January 1909. National State Bank was on the southwest corner and Boulder National Bank on the northwest. Recognizable on the south side are the iron-fronted Jordinelli and Fonda Buildings and the Boettcher Building west of 12th Street (Broadway). On the north side, note the Macky Building, the bay windows of the Rogers Block, and the large flagpole on top of the White-Davis Building. Photo ca. 1909. *Carnegie Branch Library for Local History, Boulder Historical Society Collection.*

Jennifer Schrader and David Bailey, of the University of Colorado ski team, demonstrated skiing techniques during a promotion for the National State Bank expansion shortly after the pedestrian mall opened in 1977. *Photo by Jerry Cleveland, 1977. Carnegie Branch Library for Local History, Boulder Historical Society Daily Camera Collection.*

NAT LYON POST. No.5   BOULDER, COL.

The Nathaniel Lyon Post 5 of the Grand Army of the Republic, an organization of Union Civil War veterans, posed in front of the southeast corner of 13th and Pearl Streets. Miller and Company advertised "cash for hides," and Horace Booth sold groceries. Note the flat false fronts of the buildings. Photo ca. 1880s. *Carnegie Branch Library for Local History, Boulder Historical Society Collection.*

The Saller Dry Goods store was built on this location in 1920. The banner to the left of the store advertised Cheyenne Frontier Days. The age of the automobile had arrived, and 13th Street as well as Pearl was paved. Photo 1924. *Carnegie Branch Library for Local History, Boulder Historical Society Collection.*

Saller's burned down in 1928, and the J. C. Penney Company's store was built in its place two years later. Penney's remained until 1962. In 1966, the building was extensively remodeled as the Homestead Associates Office Building. It was remodeled again in 1982 with a new brick exterior. The Mountaineer Shop Building, on the left, housed Fred's Restaurant from 1969 to 1985. Photo ca. 1949. *Carnegie Branch Library for Local History, Boulder Historical Society Collection.*

Now Rocky Mountain Chocolate Factory and Crystal Galleries are at this location. The bank building is in the background. *Photo by author, 2005.*

The north side of Pearl Street between 13th and 14th Streets borders Court House Square. The original Victorian-style Boulder County Court House was built in 1882 for a total cost of $59,950. This early photo shows it decorated for Christmas. *Carnegie Branch Library for Local History, Boulder Historical Society Daily Camera Collection.*

The original court house burned on February 9, 1932. All available firemen battled the blaze. Employees carried out most of the documents, and prisoners jailed in the basement were transferred to Longmont. *Photo by Charles F. Snow, 1932. Carnegie Branch Library for Local History, Boulder Historical Society Collection.*

Flames started in the cupola. An hour later, the 700-pound clock and 5 tons of sand used as a weight crashed through the structure and spread the fire to the second floor. Boulder's Civil War statue, "In Memory of Our Honored Dead," kept watch. *Photo by Charles F. Snow, 1932. Carnegie Branch Library for Local History, Boulder Historical Society Collection.*

After the fire, which destroyed the interior, the brick walls of the original building were torn down. The new Art Deco–style court house, designed by architect Glen H. Huntington, was built on the same foundation and completed in 1933. Stone for its façade came from bridge foundations abandoned by the Denver Boulder & Western narrow-gauge railroad. Since this photo was taken in 1993, the Civil War statue has been moved to another location on the court house lawn. *Photo by author, 1993.*

Pat Putney, as "Miss Merry Christmas," and Sam Downs, as "Santa Claus," posed with Emil Johnson and Frank S. Henderson in front of the new court house. Photo 1950. *Carnegie Branch Library for Local History, Boulder, Chamber of Commerce Collection.*

Christmas decorations on the new court house were extensive, if not outright gaudy. Compare the decorations with those on the old court house. Photo 1960. *Carnegie Branch Library for Local History, Boulder, Chamber of Commerce Collection.*

Although sparse in ornamentation, the new court house featured a frieze of a miner and a farmer over the main entrance. Mining and farming were still Boulder County's main occupations in the 1930s.
Photo by author, 1993.

The main building of today's court house looks as it did when completed in 1933. In 1961, a jail building was added on the west side. In 1962, the Hall of Justice was built to the east. When the Justice Center, at 6th Street and Canyon Boulevard, was opened in 1976, the jail and many of the courtrooms were moved, allowing court house offices to expand. The monument on the right honors Boulder's World War I veterans.
Photo by author, 2005.

The northeast corner of 14th and Pearl Streets was the site of the first frame house in Boulder, built in 1860 by Andrew J. Macky. After it was torn down, Louis Ehrlich built his first Ehrlich Block, which contained the Van Slykes store selling ladies' and children's clothing. On the second floor was photographer Ed Tangen's studio. *Photo by Ed Tangen, 1928. Carnegie Branch Library for Local History, Boulder Historical Society Collection.*

Casey School's Marching Band paraded past Kahn's Ladies' Wear in the remodeled Ehrlich Building. To the east were Don's Shop (men's clothing), the Singer Sewing Machine store, and Montgomery Ward. Photo 1949. *Carnegie Branch Library for Local History, Boulder, Daily Camera Collection.*

Parents took their children to see Santa Claus, who waited on a platform in front of the court house. The loudspeakers in the foreground were mounted on the Boulder Radio and Television Center's truck. Kahn's Ladies' Wear and a view east on Pearl Street are in the background. Photo 1951. *Carnegie Branch Library for Local History, Boulder Historical Society Collection.*

An entirely new building, the Crystal Center, has occupied the Kahn's location since the mid-1980s. *Photo by author, 2005.*

The Masonic Temple Building, on the southwest corner of 14th and Pearl Streets, was built in 1895. By 1901, it contained a drug store as well as a billiards and pool room, a bakery, a real estate and insurance business, a dentist, a jeweler, six lawyers, the Colorado Telephone Company, five Masonic groups, and Maria Tourtellot, optician. The Union Pacific Depot, built in 1890, is at the far left in the background. Photo ca. 1899. *Carnegie Branch Library for Local History, Boulder Historical Society Collection.*

Participants in the Lions Club bicycle race paused in front of Temple Drug, where Chamber of Commerce secretary Eben G. Fine was pharmacist. *Photo by Ed Tangen, 1921. Carnegie Branch Library for Local History, Boulder Historical Society Collection.*

Walgreens had replaced Temple Drug in the corner storefront. In April 1945, the Masonic Temple Building burned beyond repair and was torn down. Four years later, Walgreens reopened at the same location in a much more modest building. Janet's (clothing) Shops was next door. Photo 1949. *Carnegie Branch Library for Local History, Boulder Historical Society Collection.*

Now Lazy Dog Sports Bar & Grill occupies the former Walgreens and Janet's stores. *Photo by author, 2005.*

The clock on the court house read 10:15 a.m. on a cold winter day when this photo was taken. Dominating the scene is the original Boulder County Court House, complete with a flag and flagpole on top of the cupola. The Masonic Temple Building is on the southwest corner of 14th and Pearl Streets. Across 14th Street is the Sullivan Building. To the left of the court house is the Boulder National Bank Building. To the right is the Elks Club, also with a tall flagpole, and the Hotel Boulderado. Bands performed on top of the little building on the Spruce Street side of the court house. A coal and wood smoke haze hung over the city. *Photo by Ed Tangen, 1920. Carnegie Branch Library for Local History, Boulder Historical Society Collection.*

A 1993 comparison shows the new court house, with straight, rather than curved, walkways. The Masonic Temple Building was replaced with Walgreens, which was Rocky Mountain Records and Tapes (now Lazy Dog Sports Bar & Grill) when this photo was taken. On the left on 14th Street is the Colorado Building. The Boulder National Bank Building is visible across 13th Street, but the Pearl Street mall is obscured by trees. *Photo by author, 1993.*

Mickey Mouse brightened up Pearl Street as a Christmas decoration in 1936. Wayne's Café, on the northwest corner of 15th and Pearl Streets, was in the background. On the southeast corner was McAllister Lumber and Supply Company. In the distance, behind the pole, was State Preparatory School, at 17th and Pearl Streets. *Carnegie Branch Library for Local History, Boulder Historical Society Collection.*

Groceries were neatly displayed in Skagg's Safeway in the Sullivan Building, on the southeast corner of 14th and Pearl Streets. *Photo by Ed Tangen, 1929. Carnegie Branch Library for Local History, Boulder Historical Society Collection.*

Marion Skaggs founded the first Safeway store in American Falls, Idaho, in 1915. He operated on the basis of his new concept of "cash and carry," instead of extending credit, and losing money, as previous grocers had done. Delivery trucks lined up along 14th Street. The Van Slykes store is in the background across Pearl Street. *Photo by Ed Tangen, 1928. Carnegie Branch Library for Local History, Boulder Historical Society Collection.*

Today, "Sullivan" has been removed from the pediment. Note the distinctive lintels with keystones over the windows. Now Hurdle's Jewelry and the 14th Street Bar and Grill occupy the building. The Crystal Center is in the background on the left. *Photo by author, 2005.*

During the pre-mall era, the brick had been painted on the Sullivan Building. Next door was the Boulder Hardware Building, with its distinctive cast-iron facade. Photo 1975. *Carnegie Branch Library for Local History, Boulder, Communication Arts Collection.*

The trees on Pearl Street are almost a forest. Hidden behind them is Hurdle's Jewelry, still located in the Sullivan Building. The interpretive sign in the foreground is one of twelve historical panels on the Pearl Street mall. *Photo by author, 2005.*

The Big Snow ~ Dec. 4, 5, 1913 ~ 1400 Block on Pearl

A big snowstorm on December 4 and 5, 1913, left the 1400 block of Pearl Street impassable. Electric lines for the Denver and Interurban Railroad ran overhead, although the only vehicles to get through were sleighs. Citizens National Bank was on the left. The Masonic Temple Building, on the southwest corner of 14th and Pearl Streets, was in the background. Photo 1913. *Carnegie Branch Library for Local History, Boulder Historical Society Collection.*

The Citizens National Bank Building and other buildings on the south side of Pearl Street between 14th and 15th Streets are basically the same. *Photo by author, 2005.*

Carver Brothers Motor Company was located on the southwest corner of 15th and Pearl Streets. The Citizens National Bank was in the background. *Photo by Ed Tangen, 1927. Carnegie Branch Library for Local History, Boulder Historical Society Collection.*

A new building now occupies this site. *Photo by author, 2005.*

CHAPTER THREE

SOUTH-CENTRAL BOULDER
FLOODS, MINORITIES, AND RAILROADS

The 100-year flood hit Boulder in 1894. Most of Boulder's "red light district," which covered the area along Water Street (Canyon) between the current Municipal Building and the Boulder Public Library auditorium, was destroyed. Madams blatantly moved their girls to upstairs rooms in the downtown business district. However, the brothels' days were numbered. When the Better Boulder Party succeeded in closing Boulder's saloons in 1907, it closed the "houses of ill repute" for good.

The Goss and Grove Street neighborhood, known as Culver's Subdivision, did little better in the flood. The neighborhood was home to most of the city's minorities and immigrants. A reporter, typical of his era, wrote in the *Boulder County Herald* in 1883 of the "rustic Queen Anne style come-mighty-near-tumbling-down residences of our happy-go-lucky colored population." The 1880 census listed blacks as approximately 1 percent of a population of 3,069 for the entire county. Although

the neighborhood surrounding Goss and Grove Streets was rebuilt, the majority of large homes, churches, and public buildings erected after the flood were located north of downtown or on higher ground.

Minorities were part of Boulder's history, but they are rarely pictured. Chinese placer miners kept to themselves in mountain communities. Few blacks or Asians hired photographers to have their portraits taken. Photos of Boulder prostitutes were even rarer.

In order to prosper and grow, Boulder needed the railroad. Before 1873, the coal-mining town of Erie was the closest station. It was a long wagon ride away to reach additional markets for Boulder's farmers. Two years before, Boulder residents had raised $45,000 in subscriptions to bring the Denver & Boulder Valley from Erie to Boulder. Ground was broken in 1871, "amid many toots and speeches," but the railroad company delayed construction.

On April 5, 1873, before the Denver & Boulder Valley arrived, the Colorado Central reached Boulder. The Colorado Central built a small depot, at approximately 31st and Pearl Streets, where the tracks intersected. At the time, the Colorado Central ran between Longmont and Black Hawk.

The Denver & Boulder Valley finally reached Boulder on September 10, 1873. It built a depot just north of Pearl Street between 22nd and 23rd Streets.

By 1877, both railroads were turning around at the wye, where the tracks intersected, and backing in to the Denver & Boulder Valley depot. In a little more than three hours, travelers could get to Denver on either railroad. The fare was $2.25 each way. From 1877 to 1888, a short feeder line, the Golden, Boulder & Caribou, brought coal from the Marshall coal fields to Valmont.

The two East Boulder depots were just the beginning of railroad activity in Boulder. In the years to come, Boulder would have five more depots. Meanwhile, mining activity in the mountains required a cost-effective way to bring in coal for steam-powered machinery and to haul out gold and silver ore. In 1883, the narrow-gauge Greeley, Salt Lake & Pacific connected Boulder with Sunset, then called Penn Gulch, in Four Mile Canyon.

The Greeley, Salt Lake & Pacific built Boulder's third depot just northwest of the railroad tracks and 10th Street. It was a red-frame building used for both passengers and freight for all of the railroads. The Denver & Boulder Valley depot was abandoned. Rails from the wye paralleled Pearl, then cut diagonally southwest (west of today's 28th Street) and intersected Water Street (Canyon) at 22nd Street. All trains then came into Boulder from the wye, and followed Water Street (Canyon) to the Greeley, Salt Lake & Pacific depot. Spur lines and a switching yard were built as industries de-

veloped between this depot at 10th Street and the Colorado State Flour Mill (Yount/McKenzie) near the mouth of Boulder Canyon.

From this depot, the Greeley, Salt Lake & Pacific narrow-gauge crossed Boulder Creek near 4th Street to go into the mountains. The railroad then followed what is now Arapahoe Avenue into Boulder Canyon and turned into Four Mile Canyon. Today's bike path in Boulder Canyon follows this railroad grade.

The flood of 1894 washed out many of the mountain tracks and bridges. Four years later, the narrow-gauge was reorganized as the Colorado & Northwestern, and a branch north from Sunset to Ward was built. The scenic line became known as the "Switzerland Trail of America."

In 1904, the Switzerland Trail branched south from Sunset to the latest gold-mining boomtown of Eldora. The Colorado & Northwestern sold out to the Denver, Boulder & Western in 1909. This was shortly after the beginning of Boulder's prohibition, but excursionists, often with a whole boxcar loaded with kegs of beer on ice, nicknamed the "DB&W" the "drink beer and wine." Others called it the "damned better than walking." Whatever its name, the narrow-gauge was beloved by both tourists and residents. In mining, however, the industry it was built to serve, the railroad just couldn't compete with a new invention—the truck. Financial problems and another flood, in 1919, ended the line.

A disgruntled railroad employee set fire to a boxcar at the Greeley, Salt Lake & Pacific depot in 1907. The boxcar contained 2,400 pounds of dynamite intended for the Boulder County Mine at Cardinal, between Nederland and Caribou. The resulting explosion destroyed the depot at 10th Street and blew out almost all of the windows in downtown Boulder.

Back on the plains, the Denver, Marshall & Boulder Railroad had built a line in 1886 between Boulder and Argo, the location of the Boston & Colorado Smelting Works just north of Denver. Trains hauling out gold and silver ore picked up coal at the Marshall coal fields on their return to Boulder. These trains passed through the University of Colorado campus and crossed Boulder Creek near 11th Street. (Their route is explained in Chapter 8.) A small station was built on the site of the Duane Physics Building.

The most well-known of Boulder's depots was its fourth, built by Union Pacific in 1890 at the intersection of 14th and Water (Canyon) Streets. The dedication included a band, a banquet, and dancing until late into the night. Although partially under water in the 1894 flood, the depot withstood the storm well. This sizable stone building became the passenger depot for all of the trains. The Greeley, Salt Lake & Pacific depot, before its explosion in 1907, was used for freight.

Distinguished guests arrived at the Union Pacific depot. In 1900, presidential candidate William McKinley and his running mate, Theodore Roosevelt, made campaign speeches from their train. Rival candidate, the "silver-tongued orator" William Jennings Bryan, took a carriage from the depot to the newly built Chautauqua Auditorium. Bryan lost to McKinley, but Roosevelt became president a year later when McKinley was assassinated. Roosevelt was then re-elected in 1904.

Vice-presidential candidate Franklin D. Roosevelt, who ran and lost with James M. Cox, arrived at the depot in 1920. A *Daily Camera* reporter noted that after Roosevelt's speech at the Curran Theatre, he "broke existing speed records" by eating a multicourse dinner at the Hotel Boulderado in just thirteen minutes. He then rushed back to his waiting train. Roosevelt later served three presidential terms.

Denver & Boulder Valley trains, which were controlled by Union Pacific, followed the rails east out of Boulder and connected with main north-south lines at Brighton. In 1890 the Denver, Marshall & Boulder and the Colorado Central were consolidated into the Union Pacific Denver & Gulf Its trains, which ran between Denver and Fort Collins, continued to use the route through the university.

In 1898, the Union Pacific Denver & Gulf was succeeded by the Colorado & Southern. Beginning in 1908, it operated as a subsidiary of the Chicago, Burlington & Quincy. In 1910, three years after the Greeley, Salt Lake & Pacific depot had exploded, the Colorado & Southern built a freight depot just northwest of the railroad tracks and 12th Street (Broadway).

The Denver & Interurban, controlled by the Colorado & Southern, had begun its electric rail service between Denver and Boulder in 1908. Until 1917, the impressive green train, one to three railroad cars, was like a large streetcar. It ran on Pearl Street between the wye at Boulder Junction and its depot, which was on the west side of the First National Bank at 12th (Broadway) and Pearl Streets.

Denver & Interurban trains, which left on the half hour, then continued south on 12th Street (Broadway) to follow the Colorado & Southern tracks through the university. The trains alternated between the route through the university and Marshall and the route down Pearl Street to Louisville before heading in or out of Denver.

The electric trains, which ran sixteen times a day, were cheap, clean, and efficient. A coal-fired power plant in Lafayette supplied the electricity for the overhead lines. All of the Colorado & Southern trains and half of the Denver & Interurban routes continued to go through the university. Between 1905 and 1916, this route was three-railed so that the narrow-gauge trains from the mountains could continue on to Denver.

In 1917, the downtown section of Pearl Street was paved, and the tracks were removed. The Denver & Interurban then followed the conventional rail route through east-central Boulder and stopped at the Union Pacific depot.

Because of the popularity of the automobile, the last Denver & Interurban electric train left Boulder in 1926. The Colorado & Southern trains through campus ceased in 1932. The tracks and the station on university property were removed. Without the "loop," trains backed and turned around at the wye at Boulder Junction as they had years before. Colorado & Southern trains heading south went through Louisville to Denver. Those heading north went through Longmont on their way to Cheyenne.

The Union Pacific tracks still intersected the Colorado & Southern tracks at the wye. Prior to 1941, gasoline-powered McKeen motor cars ran on the tracks between Boulder and Brighton.

Regular passenger service to the Union Pacific depot was discontinued in 1951. There just weren't enough passengers. One of the railroad fans making that last trip was University of Colorado professor John B. Schoolland. It must have been quite a contrast to the years when the Denver & Interurban ran sixteen trains a day to Denver, in addition to the Colorado & Southern and the Union Pacific trains and the narrow-gauge railroad coming out of the mountains.

Beginning in 1952, the depot housed the Travel Center and was the station for the Denver Boulder Bus Company, successor to the Denver & Interurban Motor Company. Limited train service, which brought in the mail, continued until 1957. The last railroad tracks in the city limits were removed in 1960. Water Street was renamed Canyon Boulevard in 1962. The freight depot at 12th Street (Broadway) was demolished in 1963.

Meanwhile, in 1957 the Colorado & Southern had opened a small combination passenger and freight depot, Boulder's seventh, northwest of the wye between Pearl Street and Valmont Road. Passenger service was discontinued in 1967. In 1970, the Chicago, Burlington & Quincy, which controlled the Colorado & Southern, merged with the Great Northern and the Northern Pacific Railroads, forming the Burlington Northern.

The Colorado & Southern became a subsidiary of the Burlington Northern and was merged into the Burlington Northern on December 31, 1981. Their depot was in use until 1985. The building is still there, owned and used by Sutherlands Lumber as a shop and as storage. Automobile traffic on Pearl Street and Valmont Road east of 30th Street still stops for the Burlington Northern freight trains.

In 1973, the city of Boulder opened the intersection of 14th Street and Canyon Boulevard, where the Union Pacific had built its depot in 1890. To save it from demolition, the Boulder Jaycees moved it to open space on the Pow Wow grounds, northwest of the intersection of 30th and Pearl Streets.

Although the Union Pacific depot is only a block away from the location of Boulder's first and last depots, it is surrounded by the Crossroads Commons shopping center and movie complex and has lost its historic context. Its future is uncertain.

RAILROAD DEPOTS IN BOULDER

Name of Depot	Location	Dates
Colorado Central (demolished)	Approximately 31st and Pearl Streets	1873 to ca. 1876
Denver & Boulder Valley (demolished)	Pearl Street between 22nd and 23rd Streets	1873 to 1883
Greeley, Salt Lake & Pacific (destroyed in explosion)	Water Street (Canyon) west of 10th Street	1883 to 1907
Union Pacific (used by Denver & Interurban Railroad, 1917–1926, moved to Pow Wow grounds, northwest of 30th and Pearl Streets, in 1973)	Water (Canyon) and 14th Streets	1890 to 1973
Colorado & Southern (demolished)	Water (Canyon) and 12th Streets	1910 to 1963
Denver & Interurban (was on west side of second building of First National Bank)	Pearl and 12th Streets	1908 to 1917
Colorado & Southern #2 (still standing, property of Sutherlands Lumber Company)	3400 31st Street	1957 to 1985

The buildings on the left, on the northwest corner of 12th (Broadway) and Walnut Streets, were used by Boulder's first fire department. Next door was Klette's Saloon, with a brothel upstairs. Jacob Faus's Blacksmithing, formerly E. J. Perren's farm implements, was to the right, at 1921 12th Street. In the background is the roof of the Sternberg Flour Mill. *Photo by Joseph Bevier Sturtevant, ca. 1890s. Carnegie Branch Library for Local History, Boulder Historical Society Collection.*

An office building and retail shops have replaced the former businesses. Photographer Charles F. Snow had his studio at 1909 Broadway for many years. The Randolph Center is on the left, and the Exeter Office Building is in the background. Only the mountain backdrop hasn't changed. *Photo by author, 2005.*

The Riverside Candy Kitchen, at 1718 12th Street (Broadway), advertised Coca-Cola, which was bottled across the street. In 1936, the building became the studio of photographer D. L. Yocum. His sign is still painted on the south side. Note the double streetcar tracks in the foreground. Photo ca. 1923–1926. *Carnegie Branch Library for Local History, Boulder Historical Society Collection.*

The streetcars were discontinued in 1931, but the brick building on the left is still there. The view up Broadway (formerly 12th Street) is similar. *Photo by author, 2005.*

Ca. 1900, D. C. "Clint" Fonda, youngest brother of pharmacist George F. Fonda, opened the Boulder Bottling Works at 1769 12th Street (Broadway), the storefront on the far left. In 1923, the name was changed to Coca-Cola Bottling Company and in 1940 to the Fonda–Dr. Pepper Bottling Company. In the foreground are standard- and narrow-gauge railroad tracks with the sign "Look Out for the Cars." *Photo by Joseph Bevier Sturtevant, ca. 1900. Carnegie Branch Library for Local History, Boulder Historical Society Collection.*

Now the Municipal Building, completed in 1952, occupies the southwest corner of 12th (Broadway) and Water (Canyon) Streets. The new building replaced city hall, which was on the west side of 14th Street between Walnut and Pearl Streets. *Photo by author, 2005.*

Two more commercial buildings were built between the Boulder Bottling Works and Boulder Creek. The one on the end, with the woman standing in front, was one of the last of several studios of photographer, Joseph Bevier Sturtevant. A prolific photographer, he took many of the pre-1910 photos of Boulder. In this photo looking north, the Boulder Bottling Works is the building with the high windows and the little girl standing in front. Photo ca. 1901. *Carnegie Branch Library for Local History, Boulder Historical Society Collection.*

This view shows another building similar to the one Sturtevant used as his studio. The Bottling Company Building became the Travis Agency for real estate, insurance, and loans. The Colorado & Southern freight depot, demolished in 1963, is in the background on the northwest corner of Broadway and Water Street (Canyon). Photo ca. 1949–1950. *Carnegie Branch Library for Local History, Boulder Historical Society Collection.*

In 1893, the Seventh Day Baptists began construction of their church on the southeast corner of 12th Street (Broadway) and Arapahoe Avenue. The partially completed building washed away in the flood the next year. The church was rebuilt on the same location. Members of Trinity Lutheran Church also worshipped in the building before the completion of their own church in 1929. Photo ca. 1897. *Carnegie Branch Library for Local History, Boulder, Wheeler Collection.*

The church was demolished in 1930 to make room for Tiny Hall's Texaco Service Station, which faced the intersection on an angle, presumably for more exposure. Photo ca. 1938. *Carnegie Branch Library for Local History, Boulder Historical Society Collection.*

Another view shows cars being serviced in the bays. Photo ca. 1938. *Carnegie Branch Library for Local History, Boulder Historical Society Collection.*

Today's retail businesses are in the same service station building. The right side has been drastically remodeled, but the doors and windows on the left merely replaced the garage doors to the bays. It's still obvious on the pavement where the cars drove in. *Photo by author, 2005.*

In 1942, a year after Safeway built a store on the southeast corner of 17th and Pearl Streets, it built another identical store on the southwest corner of Arapahoe Avenue and Broadway. Both featured modern glass windows and a parking lot. From 1958 through the 1970s, the building was owned by the Boulder Historical Society and operated as its Pioneer Museum. Photo ca. 1942. *Carnegie Branch Library for Local History, Boulder Historical Society Collection.*

Wild Oats Market is now in the old Safeway building. Although the windows have been changed and the entrance has been moved to the northwest corner, the distinctive brickwork (although a little harder to see) is still the same. *Photo by author, 2005.*

Boulder's beer was brewed at 954 Arapahoe Avenue in the Boulder City Brewery, which was built in 1876 by Frank Weisenhorn and Charles Voegtle. In 1891, they sold out to Samuel Pells, and the name was changed to Crystal Springs Brewery and Ice Company. Although the sale of alcoholic beverages was outlawed in Boulder in 1907, the brewery continued in operation until Colorado prohibition in 1916. The building burned down in 1921. Photo ca. 1880s. *Carnegie Branch Library for Local History, Boulder Historical Society Collection.*

Only a shady lane remains of the site of the once busy brewery. It was up the road from the intersection of Lincoln Place and Arapahoe Avenue, across Arapahoe from the Boulder Public Library. *Photo by author, 2005.*

The Union Pacific depot, built in 1890, was in the intersection of 14th and Water (Canyon) Streets. During the 100-year flood, the new depot was partially submerged in water from Boulder Creek. *Photo by Lawrence P. Bass, 1894. Carnegie Branch Library for Local History, Boulder Historical Society Collection.*

Friends and families welcomed home Boulder troops from the Philippines after the Spanish-American War. Three had died, but eighty-two men returned. The *Boulder News* reported that "the train rolled in amid the screaming of whistles, ringing of bells, waving of handkerchiefs, and glad shouts" and that "the boys were seized, shaken, hugged, kissed, and cheered until they were wearied and sore." The tracks for the train from Denver crossed Boulder Creek at 11th Street and pulled into the depot from the southwest. *Photo by Joseph Bevier Sturtevant, 1899. Carnegie Branch Library for Local History, Boulder Historical Society Collection.*

A woman handed a soldier an ice cream cone at the Union Pacific depot. Photo 1919. *Carnegie Branch Library for Local History, Boulder Historical Society Collection.*

The Denver & Interurbans were no longer running when this photo was taken, but the Colorado & Southern and the Union Pacific still brought in passengers and freight. *Photo by Ed Tangen, 1930. Carnegie Branch Library for Local History, Boulder Historical Society Collection.*

This view of the depot on 14th Street was taken from the new Colorado Insurance Building. The last train to arrive in Boulder was in 1957. The long building behind the tracks was the Boise-Payette Lumber Company, formerly McAllister Lumber. In the background at 1722 14th was Boulder Skateland roller rink, now an office building. *Photo by John B. Schoolland, 1958. Carnegie Branch Library for Local History, Boulder, John B. Schoolland Collection.*

Tracks were removed in 1960. Water Street was renamed Canyon Boulevard in 1962 when the street was widened to four lanes. The Denver Boulder Bus Company and the Travel Center operated from the depot beginning in 1952. Photo ca. late 1960s. *Carnegie Branch Library for Local History, Boulder Historical Society Daily Camera Collection.*

When the city of Boulder decided to reopen the 14th and Water (Canyon) Streets intersection, it planned to tear down the historic depot. Instead, the Boulder Jaycees cut the depot in half in 1973 and moved it to the Pow Wow grounds, near the intersection of 30th and Pearl Streets. Photo 1973. *Carnegie Branch Library for Local History, Boulder Historical Society Daily Camera Collection.*

The depot site is now the Canyon Boulevard and 14th Street intersection. The Colorado Building (formerly the Colorado Insurance Building and then the Vectra Bank Building) is in the background. *Photo by author, 2005.*

Central Park, on the east side of 12th Street (Broadway) between Arapahoe Avenue and Water Street (Canyon), was known in its early days as "Cigarette Park." Besides a place to smoke, it provided a cool place for these nicely dressed men to have a drink. This photo is undated, so it's not known if they were drinking beer prior to Boulder's 1907 prohibition or if they were sampling some of D. C. Fonda's carbonated beverages, bottled across the street. *Carnegie Branch Library for Local History, Boulder Historical Society Collection.*

The large cottonwoods were removed in the 1920s, the lawn was maintained, and new trees were planted. In the background, photographer D. C. Yocum had moved into the Riverside Candy Kitchen Building. The Ernest Grill Lumber Company was located to the southwest of the bridge. Photo 1936. *Carnegie Branch Library for Local History, Boulder Historical Society Daily Camera Collection.*

The bandshell was built in Central Park by the Boulder Lions Club in 1938. Here, Ogala Sioux, on a tour advertising Cheyenne Frontier Days danced for a Boulder crowd. The performance kicked off Boulder's Pow Wow Days. Photo 1956. *Carnegie Branch Library for Local History, Boulder Historical Society Daily Camera Collection.*

In 1952, University of Colorado professor John B. Schoolland led the effort to have Engine 30 (which had been sold to the Rio Grande Southern) returned to Boulder and placed in Central Park. Originally, the engine ran between Boulder, Eldora, and Ward on the Switzerland Trail, but it's currently is on loan to the Georgetown Loop Railroad. Only a plaque and caboose remain. *Photo by author, 2005.*

The impressive Boulder Milling and Elevator Company, on the southeast corner of 11th and Walnut Streets, produced its famous "lily white" flour as well as grain and feed. The mill was built by Jay Sternberg in 1889 after his first one, at 24th Street and University Avenue, had burned down. Stock was sold for the new mill at $100 a share, and most of Boulder's business community contributed. It operated until it went bankrupt in 1923. *Photo by Ed Tangen, 1921. Carnegie Branch Library for Local History, Boulder Historical Society Collection.*

Now the Randolph Center's parking garage occupies the site of the former flour mill. *Photo by author, 2005.*

The Monticello Hotel, on the southeast corner of 13th and Walnut Streets, was originally built as the American House Hotel in 1875. It became the Bowen and then the O'Connor, at which point the third story and the sweeping porches were added. It became the Miles in 1917, then the Gateway, and finally the Monticello, from 1921 until it was razed in 1955. *Photo by Ed Tangen, 1922. Carnegie Branch Library for Local History, Boulder Historical Society Collection.*

The hotel was replaced in 1956 with the new building of the Mercantile Bank and Trust Company. It changed its name to the United Bank of Boulder in 1970. When this photo was taken in 1993, the building was occupied by the Boulder Valley Bank and Trust. *Photo by author, 1993.*

The Boulder Post Office was established in 1860, with Andrew J. Macky as first postmaster. For forty-nine years, the postal service operated out of various locations in Boulder, including the Masonic Temple. In 1909, the United States Post Office, Boulder's first federal building, was built on the northwest corner of 15th and Walnut Streets. The building was added onto shortly after this photo was taken, then remodeled, and added onto again in 1959. *Photo by Ed Tangen, 1932. Carnegie Branch Library for Local History, Boulder Historical Society Collection.*

Despite the additions, the original building is easy to recognize today. *Photo by author, 2005.*

The police station (with flat roof) and City Hall (first occupied by the Phoenix Hook and Ladder Company) next door, were on the west side of 14th Street between Walnut and Pearl Streets. City offices remained until 1952, when the Municipal Building on Broadway and Water Street (now Canyon Boulevard) was completed. The DeLuxe Cab Company was across the street on Walnut but obviously couldn't resist getting two of its cars in the photo. Photo ca. 1946. *Carnegie Branch Library for Local History, Boulder Historical Society Collection.*

The old police station and city hall were razed to make room for the Colorado Insurance Building, built by financier Allen Lefferdink in 1956. Joslin's Department Store was a major tenant until 1980. For several years the building was known as the Vectra Bank Building and now is simply called the Colorado Building. *Photo by author, 2005.*

Central School, which was located on the west side of 15th Street between Water (Canyon) and Walnut Streets, was built in 1873 on the site of Pioneer School, the first schoolhouse in Colorado Territory. An 1876 addition doubled Central School's size. It held grades one through twelve until the University of Colorado opened in 1877. Then the high school grades were moved to Old Main as a college preparatory department. A monument erected in 1917 by the Daughters of the American Revolution states, "On this ground was built the first schoolhouse in Colorado in 1860." *Photo by Ed Tangen, 1919. Carnegie Branch Library for Local History, Boulder Historical Society Collection.*

In 1972, Central School was torn down, sparking the formation of the organization Historic Boulder, Inc. The school was replaced with an office building that housed the Colorado National Bank. That has since been replaced by the Westpeak Building, covering the site today. Even the monument is gone, although the plaque commemorating the first schoolhouse has been remounted on the east side of the building. *Photo by author, 2005.*

When State Preparatory School became overcrowded, the new Boulder High School was built on the southwest corner of 17th Street and Arapahoe Avenue. The school, which was dedicated in 1937, consisted of just the central portion flanked by the auditorium, the gymnasium, and the industrial arts wing. The cafeteria was on the second floor. School board members became embroiled in a controversy over the sculptures of "Strength and Wisdom," nicknamed "Minnie and Jake," over the front doors. *Photo by Charles F. Snow, 1937. Carnegie Branch Library for Local History, Boulder Historical Society Collection.*

The original part of the school looks the same. Additions throughout the years included a second gymnasium, current cafeteria, library, band room, courtyard, language and mathematics sections, and an art and science wing. *Photo by author, 2005.*

CHAPTER FOUR

NORTH-CENTRAL BOULDER
CULTURE AND RELIGION

The early part of the twentieth century was a turning point for Boulder as it grew, changed, and became a sophisticated city. Safely away from the floodplain, a number of prominent buildings were erected during this era. They include the Physicians Building, the Elks Building, and the second (and current) building of St. John's Episcopal Church, all in 1905. The Curran Theatre was completed in 1906 and the Carnegie Library in 1907. The second (and current) building of the First Congregational Church was completed in 1908. The Hotel Boulderado opened on New Year's Day, 1909.

When Isaac T. Earl was elected mayor in 1907, he determined to make Boulder "modern and progressive." Influenced by the Women's Christian Temperance Union (WCTU), his Better Boulder Party ushered in a sixty-year prohibition. Gone were the saloons as well as the brothels, forced downtown after the 1894 flood. They were replaced by a focus on culture and religion.

The WCTU, in its constant quest to keep men out of saloons, had sponsored "reading rooms" in various downtown locations. By the end of the nineteenth century, patrons wanted their own library building. In 1902, a member of the newly formed Boulder Public Library Association approached steel tycoon and philanthropist Andrew Carnegie for financing.

Carnegie agreed to give the city of Boulder a $15,000 building, under two conditions: the city had to purchase a lot, and it had to agree to maintain the library with at least $1,500 per year. The lot selected was the site of the first building of the First Congregational Church, west of 12th Street (Broadway) on Pine Street.

The Library Association approached Colorado Springs architect Thomas MacLaren for a building that would be the most perfect expression of classical architecture that the city could afford. Boulderites already called their city the "Athens of the West" and considered it "The Place to Live," as a

Boulder Commercial Association motto proclaimed. MacLaren responded that just eight months before, the Temple on the Illissus had been unearthed just outside of Athens. He suggested that the design of that temple become Boulder's first public library building. Only the best materials were used—Gunnison County sandstone, sand and lime brick from Colorado Springs, Oregon fir, New Mexico clear pine, and, for the fireplace, Vermont marble. Carnegie Library opened with three thousand volumes. Most of the patrons requested books on romantic fiction.

Besides reading, Boulderites wanted live entertainment. Silent screen actress Ethel Barrymore often performed at the Curran Theatre. So, too, did Denver-born actor Douglas Fairbanks, known for his roles in *Robin Hood* and *The Mark of Zorro.* Accompanying him was his wife, Mary Pickford, famous for co-starring with Ethel's brother, Lionel Barrymore, in the silent film *The New York Hat.*

The theater also became the center for community events, including music concerts, church plays, Shakespearean plays, and Christmas caroling. Silent films were shown for a nickel. Ten thousand drawings went into the first animated cartoon, *Gertie the Dinosaur.* When a film was shown with an approaching train, many in the audience got up and ran. During Boulder's semicentennial celebration in 1909 promoter Eben G. Fine even found time to take the visiting Utes to see the silent film *Custer's Last Stand.*

Billy Sunday, a baseball player turned evangelist, swept Boulder off its feet with dynamic sermons of hellfire and damnation. For his 1909 visit, volunteers built a temporary 100,000-square-foot wooden "tabernacle," seating four thousand, on the site of Casey Middle School. Sunday climbed onto chairs, shook his fists, and was introduced to his audiences as "the man who would ram his sword into your putrid, rotten, dirty, sinful lives." The people loved him and donated generously. The building was used briefly for roller skating before being torn down. Sunday continued to speak in Boulder through the 1930s, with his later sermons held at Chautauqua.

A number of churches are in the north-central district. Those not pictured include the First Church of Christ Scientist, at 2243 13th Street and Trinity Lutheran Church, at 2200 Broadway. The original Seventh Day Adventist Church, at 2240 Broadway, later became the Assembly of God. The Trinity Lutheran Church parking lot now covers the site.

The First Church of Christ Scientist and Trinity Lutheran Church were designed by Glen H. Huntington, despite their different styles. The original part of Trinity Lutheran, in which Huntington collaborated with architect Margaret Read, was built in 1929 in the Gothic revival style. A 1966 addition yielded a new sanctuary.

A sharp contrast is offered by the three-story First Church of Christ Scientist, designed in the classical revival style. It was built in 1926 of gray brick with white wood trim. The entry porch has four Ionic columns that support a centered gable. It is similar in design to the Temple of Athena Nike on the Acropolis.

After Boulder outgrew the library given by Carnegie, a new library was built in 1961 at Water (Canyon) and 9th Streets. The Parks and Recreation Department used the old library building for some of its classes. In 1983, the Carnegie building was meticulously restored and reopened as the Carnegie Branch Library for Local History. This research library is now a depository for books, manuscripts, documents, oral histories, and more than two hundred thousand historical photographs of Boulder County.

This early view shows the intersection of 13th and Spruce Streets from Boulder County's original court house. The first building of the First Congregational Church (center) was erected in 1868 on the site of the Carnegie Branch Library for Local History, 1125 Pine Street. Storey's planing mill and lumber yard occupied the site of the Hotel Boulderado. Photo circa 1882–1884. *Carnegie Branch Library for Local History, Boulder Historical Society Collection.*

Now the Hotel Boulderado (center) and former Elks Club Building (lower left) dominate the intersection. Still standing is the white house, left of the hotel. Part of the house (and a storefront added in 1928) is now the Sushi Zanmai restaurant. *Photo by author, 2005.*

Ed Tangen had a good view of the north-central area from the roof above his studio. On the left is the original Boulder County Court House. Behind it on the left is the Boulder National Bank; on the right, is the Elks Club. In the center is the Hotel Boulderado. The large building on the northwest corner of 14th and Spruce Streets is the Physicians Building, and next to it is the Telephone Building. On the far right is the First Methodist Church. Behind it is the second building of the Sacred Heart Catholic Church, when the church was on the northwest corner of 14th Street and Mapleton Avenue. The former Sacred Heart of Jesus School is the white building to the west. *Photo by Ed Tangen, 1920. Carnegie Branch Library for Local History, Boulder Historical Society Collection.*

A 1993 comparison shows the new court house, with the Hall of Justice, completed in 1962, on the east side. The Elks Club Building (now the County Annex) is blocked from view, as is part of the Hotel Boulderado. The Physicians Building is still on the corner of 14th and Spruce Streets. The bell tower of the First Methodist Church is barely visible on the right. In the background is the steeple of the third building of the Sacred Heart of Jesus Church. A parking lot replaced the old church and school when the Sacred Heart of Jesus School was rebuilt on 13th Street. *Photo by author, 1993.*

The Benevolent and Protective Order of the Elks 566 was organized in 1900 and met upstairs at 1427 Pearl Street while collecting subscriptions to construct its own building. After $30,000 was raised, Andrew J. Macky, president of the First National Bank, contributed $20,000 to begin construction. The formal opening of the lodge, on the southwest corner of 13th and Spruce Streets, was on March 8, 1905. The Hotel Boulderado is to the right. *Photo by Palace Studio, ca. 1910. Carnegie Branch Library for Local History, Boulder Historical Society Collection.*

Screens were added to the porch, and a roof was built over the balcony. The first floor was entered through a large central hallway flanked by a lounging room, a parlor, an office, private telephone booths, a coat room, a lavatory, a smoking room, and billiards and card rooms. The third floor, beneath the dormers, contained five sleeping apartments for members without homes. *Photo by Ed Tangen, 1928. Carnegie Branch Library for Local History, Boulder Historical Society Collection.*

A stuffed and movable elk decorated the large meeting room on the west end of the second floor shortly after the building opened. In the front of the building on the second floor were the ladies' reception rooms and the reading and writing rooms. In the basement were bowling alleys, a swimming pool, an athletic room, showers and locker rooms, a barber shop, and a boiler room. Photo ca. 1905. *Carnegie Branch Library for Local History, Boulder Historical Society Collection.*

In 1967, the Elks moved into a new building at 3875 28th Street. Glassed-in porches give more room to their old building, now used as the "Boulder County Courthouse Annex." *Photo by author, 2005.*

The Hotel Boulderado opened on New Year's Day, 1909. Several years before, City Council members had felt that with a population of eleven thousand, Boulder wasn't growing quickly enough and needed a "first-class" hotel. Building funds were raised at $100 per share. Automobiles were assembled for a road race, but the hotel still used its horse-drawn wagon to transport the guests' heavy trunks from the railroad depot. *Photo by Thomas C. Black, ca. 1913. Carnegie Branch Library for Local History, Boulder Historical Society Collection.*

The Boulder Fire Department posed in front of the Spruce Street entrance with its new 1931 American La France fire truck on the left. On the far right is a 1931 White fire truck. John W. Baker's barbershop occupied a storefront, now part of the Corner Bar. Physician Margaret L. Johnson and the Yellow Cab Company also had offices in the hotel at the time. Photo ca. 1931. *Carnegie Branch Library for Local History, Boulder Historical Society Collection.*

A society of Union veterans from the Civil War, named the Grand Army of the Republic, chose the Hotel Boulderado as the headquarters for its department encampment. Here, members posed in front of the portico at the Spruce Street entrance. In 1963, the bricks in the portico were crumbling, so it was torn down. Photo 1928. *Carnegie Branch Library for Local History, Boulder Historical Society Collection.*

Today, the original hotel building is essentially the same. The hotel was named "Boulderado" as a combination of "Boulder" and "Colorado" so that guests would not forget where they had been. Plans are underway to rebuild the portico over the Spruce Street entrance. *Photo by author, 2005.*

The Roller Rink, also known as the Rink Auditorium, was on the northwest corner of 14th and Spruce Streets. On the northeast corner of the intersection was the first building of the First Methodist Church, completed in 1872. When this photo was taken, crowds were celebrating an anniversary of the Independent Order of the Odd fellows. *Photo by Joseph Bevier Sturtevant, 1886. Carnegie Branch Library for Local History, Boulder Historical Society Collection.*

The Physicians Building, built in 1905, replaced the Roller Rink. It was designed by the Boulder firm Wright and Saunders especially for doctors' offices, with a large third floor meeting room. Next door to the west, at 1327 Spruce Street, was the Telephone Building, where the Colorado Telephone Company moved in 1904. The telephone exchange moved in 1938 to 1319 Spruce Street and then in 1953 to Qwest's current location at 1545 Walnut Street. The Telephone Building was razed in 1964. *Photo by Thomas C. Black, ca. 1920. Carnegie Branch Library for Local History, Boulder Historical Society Collection.*

Today the Physicians Building, at 1345 Spruce Street, is the Shambhala Meditation Center. It was purchased in 1975 for the day-to-day operation of the Buddhist community known as Karma Dzong. A shrine room now occupies the third-floor meeting room. In 1892, the second, and current, First Methodist Church replaced the first building of the First Methodist Church. A new sanctuary was completed in 1960. *Photo by author, 2005.*

Boulder's telephone company first opened in the Daily Camera Building with twenty-five subscribers. In 1896, it moved to the Masonic Temple Building, as phone service slowly became popular. By 1904, when it moved into the Spruce Street building, there were 913 phones in Boulder. No longer did callers have to crank their telephones to ring a bell in the telephone office to signal an operator. New technology allowed them to simply lift the receiver off the hook to get an operator. Dial service, however, was not available in Boulder until 1954! *Photo by Ed Tangen, 1914. Carnegie Branch Library for Local History, Boulder Historical Society Collection.*

The Hotel St. Julien was built ca. 1898 by Mrs. St. Julien, presumably one of the women in this photo. The management's aim was to be the "largest and best moderate-priced hotel in Northern Colorado." St. Julien died in 1906, but the hotel remained in business until 1923. Photo ca. 1900. *Carnegie Branch Library for Local History, Boulder Historical Society Collection.*

In 1966, the St. Julien Building was razed for the construction of the St. Paul Title Insurance Corporation Building, used for many years by Boulder County Administrative Services. *Photo by author, 2005.*

During World War I, the Student Army Training Corps marched south on 14th Street from the intersection of 14th and Spruce Streets. In the background is the second building of the First Methodist Church. The white bay windows were on the St. Julien Hotel, on the southeast corner. The long white building is the Pearl Block, built in the mid-1890s. When this photo was taken, the Pearl Block housed the Curran Theatre, Hartman Grocery, Curran Rooms, C. F. Snow Photography, Mrs. L. S. Schnott's Millinery, and Ideal Bakery. *Photo by Ed Tangen, 1918. Carnegie Branch Library for Local History, Boulder Historical Society Collection.*

Now the only parts of the Pearl Block that have remained the same are the storefronts under the four southernmost windows. The Boulder Theater opened in 1936 on the site of the Curran. Its Art Deco style was patterned after Boulder's new courthouse. *Photo by author, 2005.*

The Dittmer residence was on the northeast corner of 12th (Broadway) and Spruce Streets. In 1892, the family sold the house to the Boulder Club, an athletic club for men. A gymnasium was added to the rear of the building ca. 1900. Photo 1877. *Carnegie Branch Library for Local History, Boulder Historical Society Collection.*

In 1940, an article in the *Daily Camera* announced, "Boulder Club Building to be Replaced by Modern Gas Station." Woody's Texaco service station was said to be "the most modern designed and a credit to the corner." *Photo by D. L. Yocum, ca. 1948–1950. Carnegie Branch Library for Local History, Boulder Historical Society Collection.*

Today, a parking lot flanked by office buildings occupies the site of the Dittmer house and the Texaco station. The original Hotel Boulderado building is on the far right. Its addition (on the left) extends to the southeast corner of Broadway and Pine Street. *Photo by author, 2005.*

MR P W.W. WOLF, THE LARGEST WHOLSALE & RETALE MEAT MARKET IN BOULDER, COLO. CORNER OF 12ª & SPRUCE ST. J.B. STURTEVANT.

The W. W. Wolf Meat Market was on the southeast corner of 12th (Broadway) and Spruce Streets. The Wolf family raised its cattle on a ranch northeast of the intersection of 12th Street (Broadway) and Iris Avenue. On the second floor of the building to the right was the Dewey Hotel, named for Admiral George Dewey of the Spanish-American War. *Photo by Joseph Bevier Sturtevant, ca. 1900. Carnegie Branch Library for Local History, Boulder Historical Society Collection.*

Now the building contains retail shops, with the Sienna Square Building around and behind it. *Photo by author, 2005.*

Frederick White and Albert A. Reed, two of Boulder's staunchest prohibitionists, built the Willard Building on the southwest corner of 12th (Broadway) and Spruce Streets in 1898. It was named for Frances Willard, national president of the Women's Christian Temperance Union from 1879 to 1898 and also an avid bicyclist. This photo shows the building draped in Knights Templar banners. Photo ca. 1913. *Carnegie Branch Library for Local History, Boulder Historical Society Collection.*

The Willard Building, complete with turret, has recently been restored. For many years, the building's corner storefront was the home of the Aristocrat Steakhouse. *Photo by author, 2005.*

Sale Hotel ~ the present Arlington ~ on 12th between Spruce and Pine.

The Sale Hotel was built in 1876 at 2121 12th Street (Broadway), on the west side between Spruce and Pine Streets. The large brick building is visible in the photo looking northwest from the original court house. George Sale, son of the owner, told author Forest Crossen in a 1965 interview that Frank and Jesse James had hidden out in the hotel for a week. Photo ca. 1880s. *Carnegie Branch Library for Local History, Boulder Historical Society Collection.*

In 1899, the hotel became the Roberts Hotel; then in 1904 it was extensively remodeled into the Place Sanitarium. When this photo was taken, the building was called the Seven Gables Hotel, "the family hotel of repute." In front are the Pueblo Knights Templar Band and the National Guard First Regiment Band. Photo ca. 1912–1919. *Carnegie Branch Library for Local History, Boulder Historical Society Collection.*

From 1919 to 1923, the former Seven Gables Hotel became Howe Mortuary. Note the hearse parked in front. From 1924 to 1960, the building was the Arlington Hotel. *Photo by Ed Tangen, 1919. Carnegie Branch Library for Local History, Boulder Historical Society Collection.*

The Arlington, unsafe for occupancy, was torn down in 1965. Razed at the same time was Maupin's Furniture Store (built in 1916) next door at the northwest corner of Broadway and Spruce Street. The Willard Building is in the foreground. In the background is the second building of the First Congregational Church. Today the location is a parking lot. *Photo by John B. Schoolland, 1965. Carnegie Branch Library for Local History, Boulder, John B. Schoolland Collection.*

The Frank Tyler residence was built on the southeast corner of 13th and Pine Streets ca. 1902. Note the stone curbing between the sidewalk and the lawn. Photo ca. 1902. *Carnegie Branch Library for Local History, Boulder, John B. Schoolland Collection.*

In 1952, the Frank Tyler house was razed to make a parking lot for the Hotel Boulderado. The stone curbing is still there. *Photo by author, 2005.*

The second building of the First Baptist Church was completed in 1926 on the northwest corner of 13th and Pine Streets. Formerly, the congregation had met at 2036 16th Street. *Photo by Hyskell Studios, 1928. Carnegie Branch Library for Local History, Boulder Historical Society Collection.*

The main entrance of the First Baptist Church is virtually unchanged today. A separate building to the west was added in 1967. *Photo by author, 2005.*

The first service in the First Congregational Church, on the north side of Pine Street west of 12th (Broadway), was held in 1868, even though the interior was not completed. Reverend Nathan Thompson raised funds for the church bell by soliciting miners who came to Boulder for supplies. Judge Samuel M. Breath and George F. Chase, standing in front, were early Boulder settlers. Their large bushy beards were in style at the time. *Photo by J. Raymond Brackett, ca. 1880s. Carnegie Branch Library for Local History, Boulder Historical Society Collection.*

When the congregation out-grew the church, in 1905, the second building of the First Congregational Church was built across the street on the southwest corner of 12th (Broadway) and Pine Streets. It was designed by Thomas MacLaren and completed in 1908. *Photo by J. Raymond Brackett, 1911. Carnegie Branch Library for Local History, Boulder Historical Society Collection.*

In 1906, philanthropist Andrew Carnegie funded Boulder's first public library, built on the lot vacated by the first building of the First Congregational Church. The library opened in 1907. Designed by Thomas MacLaren, its classical architecture satisfied Boulder's desire to be the Athens of the West. *Photo by Thomas C. Black, ca. 1907. Carnegie Branch Library for Local History, Boulder Historical Society Collection.*

Boulder outgrew this library and in 1961 moved it to a larger building. In 1983, after years of neglect, the Carnegie Building was restored and reopened as the Carnegie Branch Library for Local History. *Photo by author, 2005.*

The first building of St. John's Episcopal Church was completed in 1879. By 1901, its congregation had outgrown the small brick building on the northeast corner of 14th and Pine Streets. Compare its architectural style with that of the first building of the First Presbyterian Church and with the Swedish Lutheran Church, which became the Foursquare Gospel Church. Photo ca. 1890s. *Carnegie Branch Library for Local History, Boulder Historical Society Collection.*

On the same location the second building of St. John's Episcopal Church, designed by New York architects Henry M. Congdon and Son in the Gothic revival style, was built. Except for the tower, it was completed in 1905. The tower, with Meneely chimes, was finished in 1921. Additions date from 1965 and 1986. The Messiah Chorale and Orchestra, under the direction of Robert Arentz, leads a sing-along of George F. Handel's sacred oratorio "The Messiah" in the church every December. This photo is very similar to the way the entrance looks today. Photo ca. 1950s. *Carnegie Branch Library for Local History, Boulder Historical Society Collection.*

There have been three buildings of the Sacred Heart of Jesus Catholic Church. This shows the second building, on the northwest corner of 14th Street and Mapleton Avenue. It was built in 1907 on the site of the first building, constructed in 1877. The first building of the Sacred Heart of Jesus School is seen behind the church and was immediately to the west on the northeast corner of 13th Street and Mapleton Avenue. Photo ca. 1917. *Carnegie Branch Library for Local History, Boulder Historical Society Collection.*

Today this location is a parking lot for the second building of the Sacred Heart of Jesus School, which covers the rest of the block between Mapleton Avenue and High Street. The lot is across the street from the third building of the Sacred Heart of Jesus Catholic Church, built in 1963 on the southwest corner of 14th Street and Mapleton Avenue. *Photo by author, 2005.*

Eugene Austin formed the Boulder Pressed Brick Company just east of the intersection of 13th and Portland Streets and at the west end of "Lovers' (Sunset) Hill." Bricks from his earlier brickyard, on 24th Street, were sun-dried and were used to build Central School, Old Main, and the George F. Fonda Building, as well as his own brick home, now stuccoed, at 1543 Pine Street. The pressed bricks made between 1890 and 1906, however, were stronger. Customers from the new location included the Boulder Colorado Sanitarium and the State Preparatory School. *Photo by Joseph Bevier Sturtevant, 1900. Carnegie Branch Library for Local History, Boulder Historical Society Collection.*

This view is from the Boulder Pressed Brick Company looking over the coal-fired kilns north to 1st Avenue (Alpine). The circle in the field had been left by a recent circus. Photo ca. 1900. *Carnegie Branch Library for Local History, Boulder Historical Society Collection.*

North Side Intermediate School was constructed just west of the site of the brickyard, visible on the extreme left. The school was renamed Casey Junior High School in 1943 in honor of Superintendent Emeritus William V. Casey. In 1909, the site was used for a temporary "tabernacle" erected just for evangelist Billy Sunday's five-week Boulder visit. Sunday preached hellfire and damnation and called Boulder "a sinkhole of iniquity crying for redemption." *Photo by Ed Tangen, 1924. Carnegie Branch Library for Local History, Boulder Historical Society Collection.*

Today the school is Casey Middle School. A playing field behind the school covers part of the former brickyard. *Photo by author, 2005.*

CHAPTER FIVE

WEST-CENTRAL BOULDER
AT THE FOOT OF THE MOUNTAINS

In the summer of 1859, a reported $100,000 worth of gold, at $20.67 per ounce, was panned and sluiced from a creek named Gold Run, near present-day Gold Hill, 12 miles west of Boulder. At the same time, miners began the harder task of prospecting for primary-source gold deposits underground. The high-grade gold ore, underground but near the surface, of the Horsfal mine supported both Gold Hill and Boulder for several years.

Then came "the slump of 1863." Gold ore farther from the surface required more sophisticated milling, and gold was lost in the processing. American Indian uprisings on the plains, including the Sand Creek Massacre in 1864, interrupted shipments of supplies. Many of the miners left to prospect elsewhere or fought in the Civil War. Others saw their future in agriculture and homesteaded farms around Boulder.

Prospectors continued to search for gold, but in Caribou in 1869 they found silver. Revenues from this new mining activity poured into Boulder. The road up Boulder Cañon (Canyon), which had gone as far as the Magnolia turnoff, was completed to Nederland to get supplies to Caribou. By November 1871, Boulder's economy was much improved, and the city was incorporated.

In 1872, gold-bearing telluride ore was discovered near Gold Hill. New mills were designed to refine it. Again, prospectors rushed to the mountains west of Boulder and staked their claims. Gold mines were discovered all over Boulder County's "tellurium belt," which stretched from Jamestown on the north to Magnolia on the south and included Sunshine, Salina, Wallstreet, Sunset, and Crisman.

Although the mining companies often had their own mills near their mines, most of the mountain mills merely concentrated the gold and silver ore. In 1883, the Greeley, Salt Lake & Pacific, the first of Boulder County's narrow-gauge railroads, was extended as far as Sunset. Eventually, the railroad branched north to Ward and south to Eldora, with a stop at Cardinal, as close as it got to Caribou. (For a more complete discussion of the railroads, see Chapter 3.)

Ore was then brought to Boulder for further refining. The Preston Reduction Works, Kilton Gold Extraction Company, Atlas Mill, Delano Mill, Marshall Works, and Boyd Smelter were all in Boulder's industrial area, along the railroad tracks west of 9th Street. During World War I, the Marshall and the Boyd plants were converted to process tungsten. The Tungsten Products Refinery and the Mann Fluorspar Mill were also in operation at this time.

Spur lines and switching yards covered the area between 12th Street (Broadway) and the Colorado State Flour Mill (Yount/McKenzie) near the mouth of Boulder Cañon (Canyon). Other railroad-accessible industries in the area included W. J. Chamberlain and Company Sampling Works, Sternberg's Boulder Milling and Elevator Company, and Zang's Beer distributors.

An ore-loading ramp was built on Water Street (Canyon) west of 6th Street on the site of today's Boulder County Justice Center. Until 1957, trucks loaded with gold, silver, tungsten, and fluorspar ores drove onto the platform and unloaded their contents into railroad cars bound for out-of-town mills and smelters.

In the early days, teamsters, with harness bells ringing, jockeyed for position along Pearl Street to go up Boulder Cañon (Canyon). Tallyhos and other stagecoaches took tourists to Boulder Falls. In 1911, the first Stanley Steamer arrived in Nederland from Boulder. A few years later, convicts from the Colorado State Penitentiary were brought in to work on the road.

The improved road coincided with the era of the automobile. Sweeping the country was the song

"Come Away with Me Lucille, in My Merry Oldsmobile." Free public campgrounds, called "auto parks," sprang up for the convenience of the motorist. One was situated along Boulder Creek at 3rd Street and Arapahoe Avenue, now Eben G. Fine Park in memory of one of Boulder's staunchest promoters. Another was at 9th and Water (Canyon) Streets near the present location of the Boulder Public Library auditorium.

Adventurers in their automobiles and tourists on the railroad were encouraged to visit Arapaho Glacier. The narrow-gauge took excursionists as far as Ward, where they could be driven to Rainbow Lakes to change to horseback for the final leg of the trip.

In another highly publicized tour, passengers got off the train in Ward, boarded Stanley Steamer Mountain Wagons, and continued on to Rocky Mountain National Park, formed in 1915. When the railroad ended in 1919, the result of financial debts and another flood, glacier tours left by automobile from Boulder.

As part of Boulder's tourist promotion, the Denver & Interurban Railroad offered a $1,000 prize to the first aviator who landed a plane on the slopes of the newly discovered St. Vrain Glacier. A lanky young barnstormer and stunt flyer called "Slim" had been giving people rides around Boulder. Slim, who turned out to be Charles Lindbergh, begged for the opportunity but was told that his plane was too rickety. No one else volunteered.

Rather than traveling around, some Boulder visitors just wanted to relax and improve their health. "Sanitary resorts" were popular throughout the country, and Boulder had one, too. The Boulder Colorado Sanitarium, completed in 1896 by the Seventh Day Adventist Church, was patterned after the Battle Creek Sanitarium in Michigan. It was billed as a resort that combined the features of a medical boarding house, hospital, religious retreat, country club, and spa in an atmosphere of reform and asceticism. People came for "refreshment of the mind, body, and spirit." Ideal guests were overweight women and overworked men.

Built at the mouth of Sunshine Canyon, the "San," as it was called, could accommodate one hundred guests. Surrounding the five-story building were a powerhouse, a bakery, a laundry, a dairy barn, and, later, a dormitory for nurses. The resort advertised Swedish massage, hydrotherapy treatments, and vegetarian foods.

When guests first arrived, they ate at the "conservative table," where meat, white bread, coffee, and tea were allowed. Then they moved to the "liberal table," where they could eat meat but not coffee or tea. Finally, they reached the "radical table," where none of these "poisons" was permitted. The guests marked their menus to keep track of calories consumed. An orchestra played while they were eating.

In order to keep everyone happy and the diet interesting, Doctor John Harvey Kellogg, back in Battle Creek, continually invented new foods. His most popular were peanut butter and corn flakes. Old standbys were granola, zwieback, graham crackers, and "cereal coffee." He devised more than one hundred foods from nuts and grains.

The San became Boulder Memorial Hospital, which remained under the management of the Seventh Day Adventist Church until purchased by Boulder Community Hospital. Now the Mapleton Center, the former sanitarium blends in with the residential neighborhood of Mapleton Hill.

Gone, too, are the noisy railroads and "heavy" industry—the mills and smelters. Boulder's economic base no longer depends on mining, and, with declining farmland, it no longer needs agriculture. "Clean" industries, including the National Institute of Standards and Technology, the National Center for Atmospheric Research (NCAR), Ball Aerospace, and the International Business Machines Corporation have attracted thousands of employees to the south, east, and north of Boulder.

The *Camera*, which started as a weekly newspaper before becoming the *Boulder Daily Camera*, and now simply the *Daily Camera*, has been located on the southwest corner of 11th and Pearl Streets since 1890. Next door at 1038 Pearl was the Boulder Hose Company 1's fire station. This Christmas view shows a star on the newspaper office's roof as well as the star on Flagstaff Mountain, first displayed in 1947. Photo ca. 1950s. *Carnegie Branch Library for Local History, Boulder Historical Society Daily Camera Collection.*

In 1963, new offices of the *Daily Camera* replaced the old, with a parking lot on the site of the original building. *Photo by author, 2005.*

Boulder's Ford dealer in the mid-1920s was the Donnelly Motor Company at 1027 Walnut Street. To the left was the Standard Machine Works. The building with the decorative circle on the roofline was the Overland Motor Express Company. In the next building to the left was the office of heating and plumbing contractor Joseph J. McCabe. *Photo by Ed Tangen, 1925. Carnegie Branch Library for Local History, Boulder Historical Society Collection.*

The *Daily Camera*'s circulation department has been built on the Ford Company's location. The Standard Machine Works has been torn down. Barely visible through the trees is the building with a circle on the roofline. The building is the same, but it has a new façade. *Photo by author, 2005.*

This hotel, across Pearl Street from the *Daily Camera,* was built ca. 1874. Ulysses S. Grant, whose U.S. presidential terms extended from 1868 to 1876, ate dinner there the evening of August 21, 1880, when the hotel was known as the Brainard Hotel. Other guests of the era included Phineas T. Barnum and many of his circus performers, among them Tom Thumb and his wife. In 1894, the hotel was named the Stillman Hotel and Café. The proprietor was black businessman O. T. Jackson, fourth from the left. Photo ca. 1894. *Carnegie Branch Library for Local History, Boulder Historical Society Collection.*

Founded by Anthony Arnett and originally the Arnett Hotel, the Brainard/Stillman was renamed the Arnett Hotel in 1913. The storefront next door was Clair's Grocery and Market. On the far right was the Kenneth MacDonald Building, originally a saloon. Photo ca. 1930s. *Carnegie Branch Library for Local History, Boulder Historical Society Daily Camera Collection.*

A. R. Hoover's Palace Billiards Hall was in the basement of the hotel. *Photo by Joseph Bevier Sturtevant, ca. 1896. Carnegie Branch Library for Local History, Boulder Historical Society Collection.*

The hotel became Keller's Inn in 1968 and then Shannon's Restaurant and Lounge. The building collapsed in 1978 during an unusually heavy spring snowfall. An office and residential building has replaced the hotel and grocery store. The Kenneth MacDonald Building, with its arched upper-story windows, remains on the right. *Photo by author, 2005.*

107

Boulder's first armory building, at 934 Pearl, was built by horticulturist John Brierley in 1898. It was the headquarters of Company H, First Infantry, of the Colorado National Guard. The troops drilled and practiced target shooting in the building. Company H served in the Philippines during the Spanish-American War and was sent to restore order during the miners' strikes in Leadville and Cripple Creek. University of Colorado dances and basketball games were held there for a number of years. *Photo by Joseph Bevier Sturtevant ca. 1900. Carnegie Branch Library for Local History, Boulder Historical Society Collection.*

The Boulder Laundry opened in the Armory Building in 1919. By then, a new armory, now used by the University of Colorado, had been built at 1511 University Avenue. The laundry stayed in the Pearl Street building for more than half a century. "CO. H FIRST INFANTRY NG C." is still inscribed on stone over the entrance. The building today contains offices and retail shops. *Photo by author, 2005.*

At the W. J. Chamberlain and Company Sampling Works, 814 Pearl Street, ores, both gold and silver, were pulverized, thoroughly mixed, and then assayed to determine their value. Miners who brought in the ore were then paid the current market value, and the ore was sacked and sent by train to a smelter. The Boulder Ore Sampling Company took over the business in 1919 and operated into the mid-1930s. It was followed by the St. Joe Mining and Milling Company and the Crystal Fluorspar Company. Photo ca. 1900. *Carnegie Branch Library for Local History, Boulder Historical Society Collection.*

Now the W. J. Chamberlain and Company Building is Lolita's Market and Deli. Stucco covers the original bricks. *Photo by author, 2005.*

The narrow-gauge Greeley, Salt Lake & Pacific Railroad built a red-frame depot on Water Street (Canyon) just west of 10th Street. In 1907, an arsonist set fire to a boxcar of dynamite. The depot, and a lot of windows in Boulder, exploded. Here the curious look over the damage. *Photo by Ed Tangen, 1907. Carnegie Branch Library for Local History, Boulder Historical Society Collection.*

For many years, the former depot site was known as the "People's Parking Lot." Now it's the outdoor patio of the St. Julien Hotel, not to be confused with the Hotel St. Julien, in business from 1898 to 1923 on Spruce and 14th streets. The intersection of 9th Street and Canyon Boulevard is in the background. *Photo by author, 2005.*

The Boyd Smelter, on the left, was built in 1874 to refine gold ore. The tall building on the right was the Delano gold-processing mill, built in 1898. Although the railroad tracks of the narrow-gauge crossed Boulder Creek near 4th Street, a spur line extended west to the Colorado State Flour Mill (Yount/McKenzie). Other spurs connected the freight depot with the rest of the industrial area. Photo 1898. *Carnegie Branch Library for Local History, Boulder, Hugh F. Watts Collection.*

During World War I, the Vasco Milling Company milled tungsten ore at the Boyd Smelter plant. North of the intersection of 3rd and Pearl Streets was the Tungsten Products' Company's refining plant and smelter. The Boyd plant was located between today's Eben G. Fine Park and the Boulder County Justice Center. Office buildings and condominiums have replaced the Delano Mill, and Canyon Boulevard has replaced the spur line to the flour mill. *Photo by author, 1993.*

Although the inscription over the door reads "1888," Mapleton School actually opened in Fred Squires's pasture in 1889. The school was alone on a barren hill north of town, just like the university's Old Main was alone to the south. Farsighted city council members had approved the name of "Mapleton" before any maple trees were planted. *Photo by Louis Meile, ca. 1889. Carnegie Branch Library for Local History, Boulder Historical Society Collection.*

The first graduating class from Mapleton seems dominated by girls. Photo 1889. *Carnegie Branch Library for Local History, Boulder Historical Society Collection.*

Schoolchildren from Mapleton planted "war gardens" during World War I and continued them after the war. This was Garden 3, directly across Mapleton Avenue from the school. The houses are still there. *Photo by Ed Tangen, 1920. Carnegie Branch Library for Local History, Boulder Historical Society Collection.*

The original part of Mapleton School looks very much the same. An auditorium was built to the west of the building in 1951. *Photo by author, 1993.*

This view of Boulder was taken from the Mapleton School tower. Farmers' Ditch, which was decreed in 1863, allowed water from Boulder Creek to flow through Boulder to farmers to the north and east. The prominent building to the right of center is the original court house. Farther to the right in the background is Central School. *Photo by Joseph Bevier Sturtevant, 1895. Carnegie Branch Library for Local History, Boulder Historical Society Collection.*

Mapleton School is in the center background of this view of what would be called Mapleton Hill. Behind is the Klinger house, built in 1891. On the far left was the Boulder Pressed Brick Company, just east of the intersection of 13th and Portland Streets. In the left center is the Duncan house, built in 1892 at 430 Hill Street (Mapleton). *Photo by J. Raymond Brackett, ca. 1892. Carnegie Branch Library for Local History, Boulder Historical Society Collection.*

Two hundred silver maples were planted along Hill Street (Mapleton) in the early 1890s. This was after Mapleton School was built and a decade before this section of Hill Street was renamed Mapleton Avenue. A newspaper editorial read, "Trees will take away the barren look, and give an air of thrift and comfort." *Photo by Joseph Bevier Sturtevant, 1895. Carnegie Branch Library for Local History, Boulder Historical Society Collection.*

The neatly planted rows of maples are now lost in a forest of trees. The prominent building in the background on the right is the Colorado Building (formerly the Colorado Insurance Building and then the Vectra Bank Building), on 14th and Walnut Streets. *Photo by author, 1993.*

The Squires and Tourtellot families moved together to Boulder in 1860. Identical twin sisters Miranda Squires and Maria Tourtellot arrived at a time when there were few women in town. Their joint house, built in 1865, was the first to be made of stone. From left to right are Abigail Phillips, Frederick L. Squires, Miranda Squires, Frederick V. Squires, Maria Tourtellot, Frank Pound, and George Squires. *Carnegie Branch Library for Local History, Boulder Historical Society Collection.*

The home (with porch removed) at 1019 Spruce Street is considered the oldest house in Boulder. *Photo by author, 2005.*

Williamette "Will" Arnett built this showcase home in 1877 on the southwest corner of Pearl and 7th Streets. The son of freighter and hotel operator Anthony Arnett, Will lost his life in 1900 prospecting for gold during the Klondike gold rush. Photo ca. 1900. *Carnegie Branch Library for Local History, Boulder Historical Society Collection.*

The Hiram Fullen family owned the house for many years. From 1993 to 2005 the Arnett-Fullen house was the home of Historic Boulder, Inc. *Photo by author, 2005.*

In the 1920s, the city of Boulder established the Boulder Auto Camp off of Arapahoe Avenue near the mouth of Boulder Canyon. The free campground provided motorists with electric lights, gas stoves, water, toilets, and laundry and bathing facilities. The shelter house is on the right. This photo was used for publicity by the Boulder Chamber of Commerce. *Photo by Ed Tangen, ca. 1922. Carnegie Branch Library for Local History, Boulder Historical Society Collection.*

The shelter house is still standing in what is now Eben G. Fine Park. Fine was a pharmacist for George F. Fonda and later owned and operated the Temple Drug Store in the Masonic Temple Building. Fine was secretary of the Boulder Chamber of Commerce from 1927 to 1935. He traveled around the country lecturing and showing lantern slides of Boulder County to encourage people to visit. *Photo by author, 1993.*

The Boulder Colorado Sanitarium was built by the Seventh Day Adventist Church and completed in 1896. This convalescent center, which was famous for its hydrotherapy treatments and vegetarian diets, was patterned after the Battle Creek, Michigan, sanitarium, where Dr. John Harvey Kellogg invented corn flakes and peanut butter. The superintendent was Dr. O. G. Place, who soon left on a mission to India and later returned to manage his own sanitarium in the former Sale Hotel Building on Broadway. *Photo by Ed Tangen, 1927. Carnegie Branch Library for Local History, Boulder Historical Society Collection.*

In 1956, the Sanitarium became the Boulder Colorado Sanitarium and Hospital. In 1957, the original building was razed. The remaining additions became Boulder Memorial Hospital in 1962. In 1972, still under the management of the Seventh Day Adventist Church, it was extensively remodeled into a modern hospital. Now the building is owned by Boulder Community Hospital and is called the Mapleton Center. *Photo by author, 2005.*

CHAPTER SIX

EAST-CENTRAL BOULDER
THE WORKING MAN'S NEIGHBORHOOD

L
ike the north-central area, the east-central neighborhood had numerous churches. Amos Bixby, an attorney, postmaster, and journalist, wrote that even before the churches were built, children were organized into Sunday schools. One was held at the home of Mr. Goss and Mr. Pell and, appropriately, was called "Gospel Hall." The black community worshipped at several rented locations until it built the African Methodist Church on the west side of 18th Street between Pearl and Spruce Streets in 1884.

Some of the historic churches not shown include the former Pillar of Fire Church, demolished November 23, 1993. It previously was the First Baptist Church, then the Church of Christ, at 2036 16th Street. The Pilgrim Holiness, and previous denominations, at 1648 Spruce Street is now a private residence. The Jehovah's Witnesses Church was located at 1831 22nd. The Second Baptist Church was sited at 1837 19th Street in 1946. The First Church of the Nazarene's building, at 1539 Spruce Street, was completed in 1925 and later became Unity Church. It is now owned by the Elim Tabernacle of Christ.

When the Denver & Boulder Valley Railroad first arrived in Boulder in 1873, it built a depot on Pearl Street between 22nd and 23rd Streets. The depot was in use only for ten years, but the "former station grounds" between Pearl and Spruce Streets, extending from 21st Street to today's Folsom Street, remained undeveloped for some time.

Before State Preparatory School was built, the "ballfield" was another open area between Front (Walnut) and Pearl Streets and 17th and 19th Streets. Boys from Central, Pine (Whittier), and Mapleton Schools played baseball games there. This area was also called the "circus grounds," as it was one of the places in Boulder where circuses would perform. They always involved parades and gave most children their first view of tigers, elephants, camels, and other exotic wild animals.

From 1883 to 1957, trains ran along Water Street (Canyon) from the downtown depots to 22nd and Water Streets. From there, the tracks turned to the northeast, where they crossed today's Folsom Street near South Street. They then crossed Pearl Street between today's Folsom and 28th Streets, paralleled Pearl Street on the north, and continued east to the wye. (For a more complete discussion on railroads, see Chapter 3.)

A spur line from the railroad ended at the Hygienic Ice and Coal Company, on the west end of the "former station grounds." In 1922, the company built a large indoor swimming pool. The building, with pool, was located on the southeast corner of 21st and Spruce Streets. A balcony was built for fashionably dressed spectators. The building and pool were sold to the city of Boulder in 1950. In 1963, they were razed and replaced with Spruce Pool. That same year, in honor of Boulder's astronaut, Scott Carpenter Pool was built near the southwest corner of 30th Street and Arapahoe Avenue.

To cheer everyone up during the Great Depression, and to unite the farmers and the miners, the Boulder Chamber of Commerce and the Boulder County Metal Mining Association initiated the Pay Dirt Pow Wow. At its first year, in 1934, there were contests for hog calling, hay pitching, pie eating, needle threading, rolling-pin throwing, rock drilling, and numerous other events. World champion rock driller Fred Dopp competed and retained his

title. A parade with floats, dignitaries, and 286 horses made its way down Pearl Street.

In 1939, a regional horse show and professional rodeo were added to the schedule of events. Many of the farming and mining contests were dropped, and the annual event became known simply as the Pow Wow. Rollie Leonard, head of the rodeo committee for many years, donated his farmland between Pearl Street and Mapleton Avenue and 28th and 30th Streets for an arena and rodeo grounds.

In 1957, the Pow Wow association was forced to give 11.5 acres to the city of Boulder in lieu of back taxes. The city developed baseball fields and gave some of its land to the Young Men's Christian Association for its new building. In 1973, the Union Pacific railroad depot was moved to part of the Pow Wow grounds to save the building from demolition. Eventually, the rodeo grounds were replaced with commercial development. The Pow Wow, renamed the Boulder Valley Pow Wow, relocated to Louisville. Without the support of the Boulder community, it was discontinued a year or two later.

Hill Street east of 12th Street (Broadway) had been changed to Mapleton Avenue in 1915, thirteen years later than the name change of the same street west of 12th Street (Broadway). The residential area today still includes a mixture of prominent homes near downtown and working-class homes mixed with commercial development farther east.

The McCapes and Lamson Livery and Boarding Stables was located at 1521–1525 Pearl Street until competition from automobiles could no longer be ignored. Photo ca. 1913–1916. *Carnegie Branch Library for Local History, Boulder Historical Society Collection.*

Nevills OK Tire Welding and Recapping Shop opened for business at the same, but extensively remodeled, location of the Motor Inn Company on the site of the livery. Trucks such as this one needed good tires when they hauled ore from the Slide and other gold mines in western Boulder County. Photo 1939. *Carnegie Branch Library for Local History, Boulder Historical Society Daily Camera Collection.*

Today, retail shops fill the space once dominated by horses, motor vehicles, and tires. *Photo by author, 2005.*

The Independent Order of the Odd Fellows was initially founded to assist miners and their families but expanded to other community affairs. The Boulder lodge was formed in 1869. Its first major project was to promote a bond issue to build Central School. In 1899, the group built the Odd Fellows Hall on the northwest corner of 16th and Pearl Streets. *Photo by Ed Tangen, 1921. Carnegie Branch Library for Local History, Boulder Historical Society Collection.*

Stained glass windows from the second-floor meeting room are visible from 16th Street. The Odd Fellows and its sister group, the Rebekahs, continue to meet. In 1980, the Boulder Army Store moved into the storefront downstairs. *Photo by author, 2005.*

The Talmage and Lilly Livery was located off the north side of the alley east of 15th Street between Spruce and Pearl Streets. Stage lines left there for Nederland, Eldora, Caribou, and Ward. Adjoining was Sam Kerr's Corral, where farmers and teamsters unhitched their teams and left their vehicles while they attended to business downtown. *Photo by Joseph Bevier Sturtevant, ca. 1897. Carnegie Branch Library for Local History, Boulder Historical Society Collection.*

The Pearl Trade Center and parking lot now occupies the site of Sam Kerr's Corral, while the Boulder Day Nursery and Hannah Barker Park (to the north) are on the site of the Talmage and Lilly Livery. *Photo by author, 2005.*

The open ground bounded by Pearl, Front (Walnut), 17th, and 19th Streets was used for baseball games and an occasional circus. This view is from 17th Street looking east. The commercial building near the center, at 1825–1831 Pearl Street, is still in use. The square brick building on the left was the African Methodist Church, torn down in 1983. Partially visible in the background on the right was the Lund Hotel, popular with Swedish immigrants. *Photo by Joseph Bevier Sturtevant, 1887. Carnegie Branch Library for Local History, Boulder Historical Society Collection.*

High school classes were taught at the University of Colorado before State Preparatory School was built in 1895. Even though "Boulder High School" is inscribed on the front of the building, the school was known as "State Prep." It stood on the south side of Pearl Street midway between 17th and 18th Streets. Jefferson Elementary School was built to the east in 1899. In 1906, an addition joined the two schools together. The complex was torn down in 1939. Photo ca. 1895. *Carnegie Branch Library for Local History, Boulder Historical Society Collection.*

1704 Pearl
Lot 5-6 Bl 72 Original Boulder

A Safeway Store and parking lot were built in 1941 on the former high school grounds on the southeast corner of 17th and Pearl Streets. An identical Safeway Store and lot, now Wild Oats Market, was built on the southwest corner of Broadway and Arapahoe Avenue. Photo ca. 1940s. *Carnegie Branch Library for Local History, Boulder Historical Society Collection.*

Safeway remained at this location until 1968. Then the building housed Liquor Mart, Nick the Greek's Music Store, Starr's Clothing and Shoe Company, and now Camille's Sidewalk Cafe. A new building occupies the old parking lot site on the right. *Photo by author, 2005.*

Pine Street School, on the southeast corner of 20th and Pine Streets, was built in 1882. It was the next school after Central School to open in Boulder. In 1885, principal and sixth-grade teacher William V. Casey inspired his students to write poet John Greenleaf Whittier on his birthday. Whittier responded, and in 1903 the school board agreed to rename the school in his honor. Photo ca. 1882. *Carnegie Branch Library for Local History, Boulder Historical Society Collection.*

Whittier Elementary (Pine Street) School is the oldest continuously used school in Colorado. From the Pine Street entrance, it looks much the same today. In 1916, an addition extended the building to the south. A more recent addition was built on the east side. *Photo by author, 2005.*

These Pine Street (Whittier) children and their teacher took time out to pose for a photographer, probably Joseph Bevier Sturtevant. The boy in the center is barefoot. Photo ca. 1900. *Carnegie Branch Library for Local History, Boulder Historical Society Collection.*

Lincoln School, at 2130 Arapahoe Avenue, is identical to North Boulder's Washington School. Both were built in 1903, when residents expected Boulder's oil boom to greatly increase the city's population. Remodeling in 1928 was done by architect Glen H. Huntington. Today, the Buddhist-founded Naropa University is located in the Lincoln School Building. *Carnegie Branch Library for Local History, Boulder Historical Society Collection.*

The first building on the southeast corner of 15th and Walnut Streets was the Reformed Episcopal Church, built in 1875. Later the small frame church was torn down and replaced by the large brick First Christian Church, which was completed in 1896. Photo ca. 1900. *Carnegie Branch Library for Local History, Boulder Historical Society Collection.*

In 1919, the First Christian Church was extensively remodeled. This photo shows the remodeled building before 1967, when it was torn down and the site became a parking lot for the First Presbyterian Church. The second building of the First Christian Church is located at 950 28th Street. *Carnegie Branch Library for Local History, Boulder Historical Society Collection.*

The first building of the First Presbyterian Church was on the west side of 16th Street between Walnut and Water (Canyon) Streets. First services were held in 1876. Formal dedication was delayed until all of the interior finish work was completed in 1881. The church was heated by a furnace under the vestibule, with a long stovepipe to the back of the building. Note the wooden sidewalks and the flagstone for stepping out of carriages in wet weather. Central School, built 1873, is in the background on the left. Photo ca. 1890. *Carnegie Branch Library for Local History, Boulder Historical Society Collection.*

A new sanctuary (now used as a chapel) and the bell tower were built in 1895. A rose window was installed in the original building. In 1907, the original building was torn down and was replaced with a two-story building facing 16th Street. The rose window was reinstalled. Additions to the west side were made in 1925 and 1956. A new sanctuary (out of view) on Canyon Boulevard was built in 1975. *Photo by author, 2005.*

Another early brick church was the Swedish Lutheran Church, built in 1895 at 2241 17th Street. It was typical of its era, with a stone foundation, brick walls, pitched roof, vestibule, and point-arched windows. Photo ca. 1896. *Carnegie Branch Library for Local History, Boulder Historical Society Collection.*

In 1956, the building became the Foursquare Gospel Church. Now it houses the architectural firm of Eric Smith Associates. The building has been carefully restored and land-marked and is an excellent example of an early Boulder church. Compare it with the first building of St. John's Episcopal Church and the original First Presbyterian Church. *Photo by author, 2005.*

CHAPTER SEVEN

NORTH BOULDER
VANISHING FARMLANDS

When homes were being built on Mapleton and University Hills, there were still farms on the north, east, and south sides of Boulder. By 1918, however, expansion had begun to creep north as Boulder gradually outgrew the central downtown area. At first, "North Boulder" was the small area north of Mapleton Avenue, east of 12th Street (Broadway), and south of 1st Avenue (Alpine). Residential areas developed, and people boarded the streetcars to shop and work downtown.

North of Alpine and east of 12th Street (Broadway) was Joseph and Eliza Wolff's fruit farm. Captain C. M. Tyler's estate, east of 19th Street, bordered part of Joseph Wolff's property.

Next to the Wolff property to the north was the Parsons' Addition. This was purchased by the Longs, who established the J. D. Long Seed Company. Farther north was the ranch of W. W. Wolf, who owned Wolf's Meat Market on 12th (Broadway) and Spruce Streets. On the top of the hill,

past present-day Linden Avenue, was the James P. Maxwell orchard. The Maxwell home is still there, west of Broadway. The large Newland Addition covered the area north of 1st Avenue (Alpine) and west of 12th Street (Broadway).

In 1953, the Boulder City Council decided that numbered streets and numbered avenues were too confusing. Instead, 1st Avenue (Alpine) and most of the numbered avenues to the north were alphabetically renamed after specific trees and shrubs.

Postwar growth in the outlying areas of Boulder created a demand for additional business districts, or shopping centers. The North Broadway Shopping Center, on Broadway just north of Alpine, opened in 1958, and the Community Plaza Shopping Center, just south of Alpine, followed in 1960.

Today, the Long Iris Gardens are the only private farmlands left in North Boulder. Residential areas have surrounded them and pushed the city limits farther north.

Knudson's North Boulder Greenhouses, famous for its orchids, was built on the southeast corner of 12th Street (Broadway) and 1st Avenue (Alpine) in 1902. The mission-style building was razed in 1959 for the Alpine Chevron service station. In 1960, Community Plaza Shopping Center was built on the surrounding property. Tenants included Plaza Cleaners, Plaza Drug Mart, Ben Franklin, Miller's Super Market, and nine other businesses. Photo 1925. *Carnegie Branch Library for Local History, Boulder Historical Society Collection.*

Alpine Chevron was torn down and replaced with the Vectra Bank of Boulder. *Photo by author, 2005.*

The North Broadway Shopping Center was ultramodern when it opened in 1958. Gene Lang's Pharmacy, Ruble's Barber Shop, Beauty Centre, Model Cleaners, Broadway Fabrics, Manual's Sweet Shop, Tasty Bake Shop, Johansen Hardware, and Ideal Market filled in the rest of the storefronts. Photo 1958. *Carnegie Branch Library for Local History, Boulder Historical Society Daily Camera Collection.*

Although under new managements, a pharmacy and a barber shop still occupy their same locations in what now is called the "Ideal Broadway Shops." *Photo by author, 2005.*

Ben Hagman, owner of the Crystal Ice Company, lived on the northwest corner of 12th Street (Broadway) and 1st Avenue (Alpine). Behind his house was a stone building where ice from a nearby pond was stored until horse-drawn ice wagons picked it up. A doctors' group bought the Hagman residence and used it as the Boulder Hospital. *Photo by Ed Tangen, 1921. Carnegie Branch Library for Local History, Boulder Historical Society Collection.*

Board president and well-known mining man William "Billy" Loach held the shovel at the official groundbreaking ceremony to remodel the former Hagman house into Boulder Community Hospital. The Crystal Ice Company's ice house is in the background. *Photo by Ed Tangen, 1925. Carnegie Branch Library for Local History, Boulder Historical Society Collection.*

The Hagman house is barely recognizable in the remodeled Community Hospital. Look closely at the front porch and the chimney behind the automobiles. *Photo by Ed Tangen, 1928. Carnegie Branch Library for Local History, Boulder Historical Society Collection.*

In 1958, the original Hagman house was torn down, and Boulder Community Hospital began a series of remodels that evolved into today's Medical Pavilion. *Photo by author, 2005.*

In 1864, Joseph Wolff home-steaded a quarter-section of farm-land between today's Alpine and Grape Avenues and today's Broadway and 19th Streets. The family's brick home was built in 1883 and designed by E. H. Dimick. It was one of the first houses in Boulder to be lighted by gas. The Wolff home faced 12th Street (Broadway) just north of what is now Elder Avenue. *Photo by Joseph Bevier Sturtevant, ca. 1890. Carnegie Branch Library for Local History, Boulder Historical Society Collection.*

An office building now separates the Wolff home from Broadway, and access is from Elder Avenue. The tree on the right is now gone, but the house has retained its character, even in the last thirty years. *Photo by Jerry Cleveland, ca. 1972–1974. Carnegie Branch Library for Local History, Boulder, Jane Valentine Barker Collection.*

In Ohio, Joseph Wolff wrote antislavery publications, but in Boulder he wrote for the *Boulder County Pioneer* newspaper and began fruit farming. At some point, he changed the name of his property from Rattlesnake Ranch to the Orchard Grove Fruit Farm. The farm was well known for its strawberries, raspberries, blackberries, grape vines, and apple trees. *Carnegie Branch Library for Local History, Boulder Historical Society Collection.*

These fawns wander freely in the Garden Homes Subdivision and enjoy fruit from the trees that date from Wolff's fruit farm. *Photo by author, 2005.*

Washington School was built in 1903 at the same time that Lincoln School, an identical building, was being constructed on Arapahoe Avenue. At the time, Boulder's oil boom, which soon fizzled, was expected to double Boulder's population. Washington School was considered "out in the country" and was one of the first buildings in "Joseph Wolff's Sub-Division." *Carnegie Branch Library for Local History, Boulder Historical Society Daily Camera Collection.*

In 1922, an addition was built onto the east side of Washington School. A prefabricated steel annex was added in 1955. The removal of the belfry was supposed to control a pigeon problem. When this photo was taken, the school had been closed, but the name "Washington Elementary School" still remained above the front entrance. *Photo by author, 2005.*

Jesse D. Long and his daughter Elizabeth posed in a field of gladiolus just south of their home at 3240 12th Street (Broadway). Long purchased the property in 1916 for his expanding J. D. Long Seed Company, a flower and vegetable seed business. Photo ca. 1921. *Carnegie Branch Library for Local History, Boulder Historical Society Collection.*

Three generations of the Long family have operated the business. Today the Long Iris Gardens is famous for its irises. Photo 1992. *Carnegie Branch Library for Local History, Boulder Historical Society Daily Camera Collection.*

The ranch of W. W. Wolf was northeast of the intersection of what is now Broadway and Iris Avenue. This Wolf raised cattle to supply his Wolf Meat Market on 12th (Broadway) and Spruce Streets. Here the Wolf family gathered for an outdoor meal by its home. Photo ca. 1916. *Carnegie Branch Library for Local History, Boulder Historical Society Collection.*

In 1918, W. W. Wolf sold his home, on twenty acres, to Boulder County for use as the County Poor Farm. In pre-welfare days, the farm housed the poor who were dependent on public relief. The residents as well as indigent outpatients received free medical care. *Photo by Ed Tangen, 1921. Carnegie Branch Library for Local History, Boulder Historical Society Collection.*

Boulder architect A. E. Saunders was hired in 1918 to remodel the house and build what became known as the Boulder County Hospital. The hospital, on the right, was to the east of the house, on the far left. *Photo by Ed Tangen, 1921. Carnegie Branch Library for Local History, Boulder Historical Society Collection.*

In 1980, the original Wolf house, used as the Poor Farm, was torn down. The former hospital building was renovated in 1973 and is still in use today by Boulder County Social Services. Compare its mission-style architecture with the remodeled First Christian Church and the North Boulder Greenhouses. *Photo by author, 2005.*

Advocates of Star and Durant cars proved their durability on the east portion of Lovers' (Sunset) Hill, now covered by houses on Alpine and Panorama Avenues and Balsam Drive. In this photo, the Star car is ready to make the 39 percent and then the 44 percent grade, which it apparently did with no problem. *Photo by Ed Tangen, 1925. Carnegie Branch Library for Local History, Boulder Historical Society Collection.*

Cars parked all along the intersection of 1st Avenue (Alpine) and 20th Street where it turns into 19th Street. In the background on the left were the farm and home of early Boulder settler Captain C. M. Tyler. He was known for raising horses, mules, and sheep as well as large acreages of wheat, oats, and hay. *Photo by Ed Tangen, 1925. Carnegie Branch Library for Local History, Boulder Historical Society Collection.*

The Captain C. M. Tyler house may look the same, but by the 1960s it had been surrounded by the new homes of the Columbine Elementary School neighborhood. This photo was taken from the east portion of Lovers' (Sunset) Hill, which was the destination of the automobiles in the "Free For All." *Photo by John B. Schoolland, 1965. Carnegie Branch Library for Local History, Boulder Historical Society Collection.*

Trees and houses currently mask Lovers' Hill. A slight bare spot to the right of center is the 44 percent grade. Both this photo and the previous one of the intersection were taken from the west portion of Lovers' Hill. The Tyler house is still standing on 20th Street but is hidden in the trees. *Photo by author, 1993.*

147

Streetcar tracks wound their way up 12th Street (Broadway), went west on 5th Avenue (Evergreen) to 5th Street, and then came back downtown. This view is looking south on 5th Street toward its intersection with 1st Avenue (Alpine). *Photo by Ed Tangen, 1926. Carnegie Branch Library for Local History, Boulder Historical Society Collection.*

The streetcars are gone, but the remodeled houses are still there. *Photo by author, 2005.*

CHAPTER EIGHT

UNIVERSITY OF COLORADO
ALONE ON THE HILL

When Jane Sewall, daughter of the university's first president, saw Old Main for the first time, she noted, "It loomed before us gaunt and alone in the pitiless clear light. No tree nor shrub nor any human habitation was in sight. Vast expanses of rock and sagebrush were its only surrounding."

There was one bonus, however: the tuition was free.

As early as 1861, residents of Boulder had decided that when Colorado became a state and had a university, it should be in Boulder. A convention composed of one delegate from each mining district was held in the territorial capital of Golden to nominate representatives to the first territorial legislature.

At the time, each mining district was a self-governing community. Gold Hill, which was formed in March 1859, was Mountain District 1, the first district in what became Colorado. The Boulder, Ward, and Sugar Loaf districts were formed in 1860. Then in 1861, the year Colorado became a territory, four more districts were quickly formed in order to get more delegates from Boulder County. All of the delegates agreed to vote for legislative candidate Charles F. Holly from Gold Hill. Holly promised, if elected, to introduce a bill to establish Boulder as the site for a state university.

Holly won and the bill was introduced. There was much discussion but little activity. Burlington, just south of Longmont, as well as Denver wanted the university, too. The Civil War was under way, the initial mining boom was over, the economy was in a slump, and the Colorado militia was fighting American Indian uprisings, which culminated in the 1864 Sand Creek Massacre.

A new university needed land and money. In 1872, Marinus G. Smith, Anthony Arnett, and George and Mary Andrews donated 52 acres on the barren bluff south of town. Two years later, the territorial legislature appropriated $15,000 for a building if the people of Boulder could match that sum. Raising the funds was a struggle because Boulderites were also putting aside money to bring in the much-needed railroad. It was said that Boulder representative and Speaker of the House Captain David H. Nichols jumped on his horse and rode from Denver to Boulder to secure pledges from Boulder's leading citizens. In the middle of the night, he supposedly rode back to Denver in time for the next day's meeting.

The first building was Old Main. It housed the entire university, including President Joseph A. Sewall and his family. Sewall had accepted the position sight unseen. The family, which came from New England, got its first view of Boulder from the train, which backed from the wye into the Denver & Boulder Valley depot off of Pearl Street between 22nd and 23rd Streets.

College preparatory school classes from Central School were held in Old Main in 1877, the year it was completed. University classes were begun the next year. There were two curricula—classical (emphasizing mathematics and languages) and scientific. Mary Rippon, a former student of Sewall's who taught French and German, arrived in 1878 and was the first woman in the country to teach at a state university. She remained until her retirement in 1909. An outdoor theater, enclosed on three sides by the Hellems Building, is named in her honor. J. Raymond Brackett, from Maine, joined the faculty in 1884.

By 1880, President Sewall had planted a few trees, while his wife, Ann E. Sewall, had planted flowers. Then Mary Rippon helped the Sewalls plant cottonwood, blue spruce, and apple trees, as well as purple lilacs and wild plums. The plum thicket west of Varsity Pond grew from that first planting. Plans for an extensive formal lawn, with well-spaced rows of trees, were abandoned in 1885

with the establishment of Arbor Day. Students and faculty were asked each year to bring any kind of tree and plant it on campus. Cottonwoods and box elders were favorites because they could be dug up and planted for free.

In the 1920s, President George Norlin decided to make the university as beautiful in winter as it was in summer. He regretted that most of the trees were bare during the winter months when classes were in session. At his request, evergreens and trees with bright berries were planted. Eastern nurseries supplied the campus with Russian olives, hawthorns, oaks, and hard maples. During his administration, the university had sixty-two varieties of trees.

Beginning in 1886, the Denver, Marshall & Boulder Railroad crossed the campus, with trains running between Boulder and the gold smelter at Argo via the Marshall coal fields. In the years to come, the Union Pacific Denver & Gulf, the Colorado & Southern, the Colorado & Northwestern, and the Denver & Interurban Railroads would all use the same track. A small campus station was located on the site of the Duane Physics Building.

The tracks came into Boulder along what is now South Broadway, over the site of the western part of Baker Dorm, then went between the Heating Plant and the Women's Gymnasium, between the Nurses' Cottage and Macky Auditorium, and then down the hill to cross Broadway between Grandview and Marine Streets. Trains then crossed Arapahoe Avenue and Boulder Creek at 11th Street and curved onto Water Street from the southwest. The tracks were removed in 1932.

Woodbury Hall, the men's dormitory, was built in 1890. It was the first building on campus with steam heat, hot and cold running water, and electricity for all of its lighting.

Each of the early buildings had its own design, and various architects were employed. Old Main, Cottages 1 and 2, the President's House, the Anatomy Building, Ekeley Chemistry, and the Hospital Building were of red brick. Woodbury Hall and the Hale Scientific Building were of stone. The Library and the Guggenheim Law Buildings were light-colored brick.

Macky Auditorium was designed by Gove and Walsh in the collegiate Gothic style. Banker Andrew J. Macky had willed $300,000 to the university when he died in 1907. Groundbreaking for an auditorium named in his honor was held on September 20, 1909. The cornerstone was laid the next year. Macky Auditorium was in use in 1912, although the interior wasn't completed until 1922. Construction was frequently interrupted because Macky's adopted daughter contested his will. The building had a seating capacity of twenty-six hundred, the largest in Boulder.

Composer John Phillip Sousa, called "the March King," with his "World-Famous Band" played a stirring post–World War I program in the unfinished Macky Auditorium in 1919. Sousa's new song, "The Golden Star," honored war veterans. Sousa played in Macky Auditorium several more times in the 1920s. Residents and students also packed the building when Helen Keller, who was both blind and deaf, included Boulder on her lecture circuit. Poet Robert Frost drew large audiences when he recited his own works. Frost often came to Boulder to visit his daughter, Marjorie, a patient at the Boulder Colorado Sanitarium. In 1986, Midyette-Seieroe and Associates renovated the auditorium and turned it into a concert hall.

The Heating Plant, also designed by Gove and Walsh, was built in 1910 and supplied all of the electricity used on campus. Coal was brought in on the train for coal-powered steam generators. The plant has since been converted to natural gas. Gove and Walsh also built the Geology Building in 1911. East and west additions in 1952 made it blend in with the surrounding buildings.

In 1918, Philadelphia architect Charles Klauder, of the firm Day and Klauder, established a rural Italian style on campus that featured red tile roofs and light and brown sandstone walls. Klauder's first design was the original part of Hellems Arts and Sciences Building in 1921. His other major buildings of the 1920s were the Men's Gymnasium (1924), Folsom Stadium (1924), two wings on Ekeley Chemistry (1926), and the Women's Gymnasium (1928), on the east side of the hospital.

After several years of fundraising, the Memorial Student Union Building (now Economics) was completed in 1931. It was dedicated to the men who gave their lives in World War I.

Federal grants provided funds during the Great Depression for several more rural-Italian-style buildings. Sewall Hall was built in 1934, the Natural History Museum in 1935, and the Balch Fieldhouse in 1936. The Women's Club Building (the northern part of McKenna), the east and west wings on Hellems, and Baker Hall were built in 1937. The Faculty Club and the original part of Norlin Library opened in 1939.

After Klauder's death, another Philadelphian firm, Trautwein and Howard, continued to design university buildings in the rural Italian style. This firm's first building was Brackett Hall in 1947. In 1953, Trautwein and Howard designed the original part of the University Memorial Center, which replaced the Memorial Building, then converted to the School of Business. The Denver firm of Moore and Bush built the 1964 addition and fountain area, now named for screenwriter Dalton Trumbo.

All planning notwithstanding, the people of Boulder didn't get the first institution of higher education in Colorado. Golden saw that honor with the opening of the Colorado School of Mines in 1874, when Colorado was still a territory. The opening of the University of Colorado in 1877 was followed two years latter by the opening of the Agricultural College, now Colorado State University, at Fort Collins.

Today, the University of Colorado has an enrollment of more than twenty-nine thousand students and nearly twelve hundred undergraduate faculty members. No longer stark and alone, the campus has many new buildings, is maturely landscaped, and covers nearly 700 acres.

The University of Colorado, which consisted of Old Main and the President's House, looked like this from 9th Street in 1886. Cottage 1, a women's dormitory, is on the extreme right. Members of the Buell family are in the foreground. *Photo by Joseph Bevier Sturtevant, 1886. Carnegie Branch Library for Local History, Boulder Historical Society Collection.*

By the mid-1890s, the university had grown, although University Hill was very sparsely populated. The prominent university buildings, left to right, were Woodbury Hall (1890), Old Main (1877), Cottages 1 and 2 (1884), Hale Scientific (1894), and the President's House (1884). Old Main, Woodbury, Hale, and the President's House all faced north to Boulder. Trees had been planted and were beginning to grow. Photo ca. 1894. *Carnegie Branch Library for Local History, Boulder Historical Society Collection.*

When the university first opened in 1877, the president's office, the family's living quarters, all classrooms, some out-of-town students' rooms, and the library were in Old Main. The Victorian-style building was constructed of bricks from Eugene Austin's first brickyard on 24th Street. Woodbury Hall is in the background on the left. *Photo by J. Raymond Brackett, ca. 1890–1893. Carnegie Branch Library for Local History, Boulder Historical Society Collection.*

Today the College of Arts and Sciences has administrative offices on the lower level and first and second floors of Old Main. The chapel has been renovated into a small theater and is used for occasional classes, lectures, and music performances. The CU Heritage Center, created in 1985 on the third floor, is an excellent museum of the university's history. *Photo by author, 1993.*

A border of silver maples was planted on either side of a wooden sidewalk between Old Main and the President's House, which was designed by Ernest Varian and completed in 1884. The buildings, from left to right, are Woodbury, Old Main, Anatomy, a horse shed, Hale Scientific, and the President's House. *Photo by J. Raymond Brackett, ca. 1894. Carnegie Branch Library for Local History, Boulder Historical Society Collection.*

Trees obscure most of these buildings today. The President's House was enlarged in 1923 and lived in until 1968. It is now the Koenig Alumni Center. A cement sidewalk replaced the wooden planks. *Photo by author, 2005.*

The Hale Scientific Building was finished in 1894 and dedicated in 1895, even though "1891" is inscribed over its entrance. It is an excellent example of Richardsonian Romanesque architectural style. The first floor was devoted to physics; the second to mathematics, civil engineering, and law; and the third to biology. *Photo by J. Raymond Brackett, ca. 1904–1910. Carnegie Branch Library for Local History, Boulder Historical Society Collection.*

East and west wings were added in 1910. The building had been named for Horace Hale, second president of the university. It was completely renovated in 1992 and now houses the Department of Anthropology. *Photo by author, 1993.*

The inscription on the law building simply read "Law School" when it was built. Senator from Colorado Simon Guggenheim, who donated funds for the building, wished to remain anonymous. By the time of the dedication on November 24, 1909, during Boulder's semicentennial celebration, he had changed his mind. Guggenheim donated an identical building to the University of Northern Colorado, in Greeley, in 1912. *Photo by T. C. Black, ca. 1910. Carnegie Branch Library for Local History, Boulder Historical Society Collection.*

Although the inscription now reads "Simon Guggenheim Law Building," the law school moved in 1959 to the Fleming Law Building in the Kittredge area. The Guggenheim Building now houses the Department of Geography. *Photo by author, 1993.*

When the Library opened in 1904 (even though "1902" is inscribed over the entrance), it was Boulder's first library building. The original campus library, funded by and named for Charles G. Buckingham, was a room in Old Main. *Photo by J. Raymond Brackett, ca. 1904. Carnegie Branch Library for Local History, Boulder Historical Society Collection.*

This interior view of the library was taken shortly after it opened. *Photo by J. Raymond Brackett, ca. 1904. Carnegie Branch Library for Local History, Boulder Historical Society Collection.*

Norlin Library, on the east side of the quadrangle, replaced the first engineering building and was completed in 1939, a year after its architect, Charles Klauder, had died. Wings were added in 1964. After the 1977 expansion, the distinctive curved windows on the east side became visible only from the inside. Over the west entrance is the inscription, first expressed by Cicero, "Who Knows Only His Own Generation Remains Always a Child." *Photo by author, 1993.*

Charles Klauder designed an addition to the west side of the original Library in 1922. He respected the original design of the building rather than his preferred rural Italian style. Now the building is the home of the Department of Theatre and Dance. An addition to the east side was built in 1982. *Photo by author, 1993.*

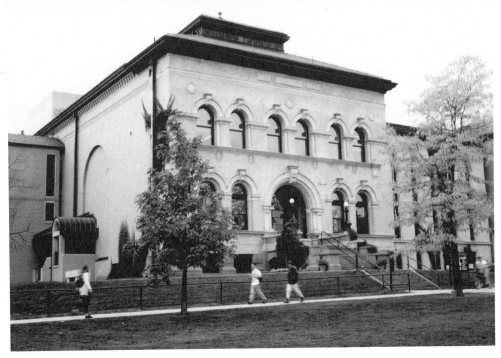

Colorado lost 10-0 in this Colorado-Nebraska football game. The athletic field had just been laid out on what was referred to as the "baseball grounds." The building in the left foreground is the 1898 part of the Ekeley Chemistry Building, which was torn down in 1972. On the right is the Anatomy Building. *Photo by J. Raymond Brackett, 1902. Carnegie Branch Library for Local History, Boulder Historical Society Collection.*

This close-up shows the west stands. Behind is the old Music Building, which was torn down in 1953 to make room for the University Memorial Center. *Photo by J. Raymond Brackett, ca. 1902. Carnegie Branch Library for Local History, Boulder Historical Society Collection.*

The University Memorial Center was built on the site of the athletic field. Inside, the Glenn Miller Ballroom honors former student and big band leader Glenn Miller. Shown here is the north entrance of the UMC and the Dalton Trumbo Fountain. *Photo by author, 2005.*

GRADUATE CLASS of 1886.

Five men and one woman graduated in the class of 1886. The men, from left to right, were Clarence Pease, Victor Noxon (grandfather of Boulder astronaut Scott Carpenter), Frederick Chase, Edward Wolcott, and Judson Rowland. Not in the photo was Helen "Ella" Tyler. Wives or sweethearts watched from the steps around the corner. *Photo by Joseph Bevier Sturtevant, 1886. Carnegie Branch Library for Local History, Boulder Historical Society Daily Camera Collection.*

This 1974 graduate, with mortarboard, shoes, and diploma, streaked across the stadium where his commencement ceremonies were being held. Photo 1974. *Carnegie Branch Library for Local History, Boulder Historical Society Daily Camera Collection.*

Many modern-day commencement exercises as well as football games have been held in Folsom Stadium. Byron "Whizzer" White, who graduated in 1938, was an All-American quarterback and a Rhodes scholar who went to Yale and became a Supreme Court justice, a position he held until his retirement in 1993. In the background is the Duane Physics, Astrophysics, and Gamow Tower complex. Photo 1974. *Carnegie Branch Library for Local History, Boulder Historical Society Daily Camera Collection.*

The forty-bed University Hospital, built in 1898, was the first hospital in Boulder other than the Boulder Colorado Sanitarium. It served Boulder residents as well as university students and faculty. *Photo by J. Raymond Brackett, 1903. Carnegie Branch Library for Local History, Boulder Historical Society Collection.*

Sewall Hall, built as the women's dormitory, is considered by many to be the finest building on campus designed by Charles Klauder. His rural Italian style featured red tile roofs and sandstone walls. Sewall Hall was built in 1934 on the site of the Nurses' Cottage just west of University Hospital. The railroad had been removed from campus in 1932. *Photo by Charles F. Snow, ca. 1935. Carnegie Branch Library for Local History, Boulder, Chamber of Commerce Collection.*

Today the hospital building is called Temporary Building 1 and is squeezed between Sewall Hall and the former Women's Gymnasium, now the Clare Small Arts and Sciences Building. The hospital was used as the student health center until 1959, when Wardenburg Health Center opened. *Photo by author, 2005.*

CHAPTER NINE

UNIVERSITY HILL AND CHAUTAUQUA
BECOMING ESTABLISHED

When Marinus G. Smith was asked by Professor J. Raymond Brackett if he would live to see the tree he was planting bear fruit, Smith replied, "Old men plant trees; young men can't wait." Smith, whom everyone called "Marine," donated part of his University Hill acreage to the University of Colorado. Marine Street has been named in his honor.

The "Hill," which looked so formidable to Jane Sewall when she first arrived in Boulder, looked a lot better with some trees. Since it was out of the floodplain, University Hill, like Mapleton Hill, became a desirable place to live. Prestigious residential subdivisions were platted and put on the market, but in the 1890s few lots were sold. One of the first went to the Sisters of Charity of the Blessed Virgin Mary who in 1892 built Mount St. Gertrude Academy, a Catholic girls' school.

Nearly two decades earlier, in 1874, a national movement had been founded to bring educational, cultural, recreational, and religious programs to communities across the country. The movement's headquarters was at Lake Chautauqua, New York. Lured by the mountain scenery and the city's cool nights, a group of Texas educators chose Boulder, specifically the 75-acre Bachelder Ranch, as the site for a Colorado chautauqua.

Only a wagon road existed to Chautauqua Park when it was established in 1898, the year of the Spanish-American War. Visitors, and their luggage, were loaded onto horse-drawn wagons after they arrived at the Union Pacific depot on 14th Street, one mile away. Opening day was July 4, with Governor Alva Adams presiding. The day was climaxed by the announcement that the U.S. Navy had destroyed the Spanish fleet at Santiago. A small city of tents, laid out like an army camp, claimed it could accommodate five thousand people.

Lectures, classes, and music programs were held in the large auditorium. Visitors ate in the dining hall for $5.00 per week, or 35¢ per meal.

Stagecoach excursions, led by none other than Joseph Bevier Sturtevant (Rocky Mountain Joe) thrilled the flatlanders. Sturtevant also led children up Flagstaff Mountain and gathered them around the campfire to hear stories of his days as an Indian scout. Groups of tourists boarded the narrow-gauge railroad, which dropped them off at Mont Alto Park, above Sunset, to pick wildflowers. Special trains then carried them on to Ward for underground mine tours. Women "tramped" in the mountains in long skirts and broad-brimmed hats.

Before the next summer season, Boulder built its first electric streetcar line. Railroad ties were unloaded at the university station and then hauled to the route that went up 12th Street, wound around University Hill as far west as 9th Street, and then reached Chautauqua Park before its return. Subsequent streetcar lines ended at the Boulder Colorado Sanitarium on Mapleton Avenue and also at the intersection of 23rd and Pine Streets.

By 1900, cottages had begun to replace the tents. Similarly, the wide open spaces among Chautauqua Park, Mount St. Gertrude Academy, and the university began to fill with homes. There were enough children living in the area in 1905 to warrant their own school, appropriately named University Hill School. It opened with six classrooms and an auditorium.

One of the earliest custom-designed homes on University Hill was George and Mildred Norlin's house at 907 12th Street. The Norlins lived in the Romanesque revival style house from 1903 to 1919, during the time George Norlin was a Greek professor at the University of Colorado. The family moved to the university's President's House when he became its fifth president.

The craftsman movement of the early twentieth century stressed comfort and utility through the use of natural materials. Craftsman homes were always two or more stories. An example of an early craftsman home, at 907 11th Street, was that of Charles Bartlett Dyke, principal of the University Hill School. Another example was the William R. Black house at 1080 10th Street. Black was a real estate broker and banker who was active in the development of University Hill.

The continued growth of the University of Colorado encouraged a second construction boom in the 1920s. Families of college students moved to Boulder, and homes were built for professors and their families. A 1924 junior high addition, called University Hill Intermediate School, greatly enlarged University Hill School.

Large fraternity and sorority houses date from this period. An example is the Pi Beta Phi sorority house at 890 11th Street, designed by Glen H. Huntington in the Jacobean-Elizabethan style. Huntington also designed several individual homes as well as the Huntington Arms apartments at 1000–1020 12th Street. The flat-roofed building was considered ultra-modern when it was completed in 1939. Also common during the 1920s was the bungalow, which was similar to the craftsman home but had only one or one and one-half stories. Bungalows have a gabled roof and a characteristic open front porch supported by thick columns or piers.

The establishment of commercial buildings in a residential area prompted Boulder's first zoning ordinance, passed in 1928. The shopping area called the Hill still caters to students. Meals, more expensive today, are still served in the Dining Hall at Chautauqua. Besides other programs, the Colorado Music Festival plays in the auditorium at Chautauqua every summer. Boulder's Chautauqua is the only one remaining west of the Mississippi River.

University Hill was a desolate place before houses were built and trees planted. University Cottage 2 is in the foreground. It was built as a women's dormitory in 1884 and torn down in the 1920s to make room for the Memorial Building, now Economics. *Photo by J. Raymond Brackett, ca. 1890. Carnegie Branch Library for Local History, Boulder Historical Society Collection.*

The Hill was just beginning to get settled when this photo was taken. The prominent building downtown is the original Boulder County Court House, to right of center. *Photo by Joseph Bevier Sturtevant, 1895. Carnegie Branch Library for Local History, Boulder Historical Society Collection.*

University Place Subdivision extended from College Avenue to Baseline Road and from 9th Street to 20th Street (then called Broadway). Here the 800 block of 13th Street was getting settled. The house to the right of the automobile is on the corner of 13th Street and Cascade Avenue. Photo ca. 1925. *Carnegie Branch Library for Local History, Boulder Historical Society Collection.*

Trees have changed the feel of the neighborhood, and the mountains have disappeared from view. *Photo by author, 2005.*

Planted trees grew well in front of some of the homes in the 800 block of 14th Street in the 1920s. The large homes to the right of center are 851 and 863 14th Street.

A sidewalk was in, but the street was still unpaved. Photo ca. 1923. *Carnegie Branch Library for Local History, Boulder Historical Society Collection.*

14th Street still has several of its early homes, including this one (second prominent house uphill in the above photograph) at 851 14th Street. *Photo by author, 2005.*

This house, on the southwest corner of 13th Street and Pennsylvania Avenue in the University Terrace Subdivision, was used by several fraternities. Note the bay window and turret. Photo pre-1928. *Carnegie Branch Library for Local History, Boulder Historical Society Collection.*

An addition in 1928 turned the building into Somers Sunken Gardens, a restaurant popular with college students. In 1959 the restaurant officially became The Sink, which had long been its nickname. It served 3.2 percent beer as regular beer, wine, and liquor were prohibited within the city limits from 1907 to 1967. The bay window is still there, but the turret is gone. *Photo by author, 2005.*

Across the street on the northwest corner of the same intersection was the Sigma Alpha Epsilon house, built in 1910 in the Capitol Hills Subdivision. Photo ca. 1920. *Carnegie Branch Library for Local History, Boulder Historical Society Collection.*

The roofline has remained the same on the former fraternity building, which now houses several businesses. *Photo by author, 2005.*

University students bought their books, stationery, and athletic goods at the University Store at 1134 13th Street on the Hill. Photo ca. 1911. *Carnegie Branch Library for Local History, Boulder Historical Society Collection.*

Now University Hill Market & Deli caters to college students in the same building. *Photo by author, 2005.*

In the 1950s, the Broadway and College Avenue intersection got so busy that it required a traffic circle. This photo is looking north on Broadway from the Chi Psi fraternity house. The Anderson Ditch is in the foreground. *Carnegie Branch Library for Local History, Central Files Collection.*

The Colorado Bookstore is now on the left, the ditch has been covered, and the traffic circle is gone. In 1992, a pedestrian underpass was built under Broadway. *Photo by author, 2005.*

The Harbeck residence was built in 1899 at 1206 Euclid Avenue. After J. H. Harbeck died in New York in 1910, the house stood vacant until 1939, when it was purchased by Milton Bergheim. *Photo by Thomas C. Black, ca. 1900–1910. Carnegie Branch Library for Local History, Boulder Historical Society Collection.*

In 1969, the Harbeck house was purchased by the city of Boulder. It's now the home of the Boulder History Museum. The Boulder Historical Society displays artifacts in the museum, while the society's photographs and documents are available for reference in the Carnegie Branch Library for Local History. *Photo by author, 2005.*

The Coulson-Noxon home, on the northwest corner of Aurora Avenue and 7th Street in the West Rose Hill Subdivision, was built ca. 1899. In the 1930s and 1940s, it was the childhood home of astronaut Scott Carpenter, who lived with his maternal grandparents. Carpenter named his Mercury Space Capsule the "Aurora 7" when he orbited the earth in 1962. *Photo by Joseph Bevier Sturtevant, ca. 1899. Carnegie Branch Library for Local History, Boulder Historical Society Collection.*

Sharp gables in the roofline have been removed, but the distinctive porch makes the house easy to recognize. Scott Carpenter Park, on 30th Street, honors the former resident. *Photo by author, 2005.*

In the early days, the Columbia (Pioneer) Cemetery stood all alone on 9th Street. The tall stone is on the grave of Truman Whitcomb, who died in 1883. Flagstaff Mountain, on the right, is almost unrecognizable without many trees. In 1927, Eben G. Fine recruited high school students to plant five-thousand evergreen seedlings. *Photo by Joseph Bevier Sturtevant, 1887. Carnegie Branch Library for Local History, Boulder Historical Society Collection.*

Trees were planted in the cemetery, and the city grew up around it. Whitcomb's tall stone (lower center) remains, although it's partially obscured by the trees. The names on the gravestones read like a "Who's Who" of Boulder. *Photo by author, 2005.*

The "Construction of the Third Flatiron—1885" was on the cover of the *Boulder Lampoon* in 1985. It was painted by Scott Knauer and made available through the courtesy of Don Koplen of the Boulder Lampoon. *Carnegie Branch Library for Local History, Boulder Historical Society Collection.*

Today the rock outcrop "under construction" is called the First, rather than the Third, Flatiron. The view is from the entrance to Chautauqua Park. *Photo by author, 1993.*

Highland School, on the northwest corner of 9th Street and Arapahoe Avenue, was built in 1892. Students posed in front shortly after completion. *Photo by Denver photographer L. D. Regnier, ca. 1892. Carnegie Branch Library for Local History, Boulder Historical Society Collection.*

Today Highland School has been preserved as Highland Offices. *Photo by author, 1993.*

University Hill School was built in 1905 on the southeast corner of 16th Street and Broadway. Its main entrance was on the west side. *Photo by Ed Tangen, 1921. Carnegie Branch Library for Local History, Boulder Historical Society Collection.*

In 1924, an addition was built onto the east side, and the elementary school was combined with University Hill Intermediate School. A band room and another classroom were added in 1929. Although the main entrance now faces to the north, this photo shows the west side today. *Photo by author, 2005.*

The Catholic girls' school Mount St. Gertrude Academy was built in 1892 by the Sisters of Charity of the Blessed Virgin Mary. It was built in a modified Richardsonian-Romanesque style. The gabled windows were removed in 1914 for renovation of the fourth floor. The school's grounds are bounded by 10th Street and Aurora, Cascade, and Lincoln Avenues. *Photo by Joseph Bevier Sturtevant, ca. 1900. Carnegie Branch Library for Local History, Boulder Historical Society Collection.*

Seventh through twelfth grade classes were taught at the academy, which encouraged a college preparatory curriculum. After 1914, several of the girls who came from outside of Boulder lived at the school. *Photo by Joseph Bevier Sturtevant, ca. 1905. Carnegie Branch Library for Local History, Boulder, Mount St. Gertrude Collection.*

Fashions changed, but schoolgirls still pursued their education. Because of declining enrollment, the academy closed in 1969. The building was sold to the University of Colorado.
Photo by James H. Roberts, ca. 1950s. Carnegie Branch Library for Local History, Boulder, Mount St. Gertrude Collection.

Two wings and a chapel were added in 1921. A fire gutted the building in 1980, but it has since been beautifully restored and is now The Academy, an upscale retirement home.
Photo by author, 2005.

When William Jennings Bryan spoke at the Chautauqua Auditorium in 1900, it was said that his booming voice could be heard as far away as the University of Colorado. In the beginning of the twentieth century, Boulder began to extend up toward Chautauqua Park. Mount St. Gertrude Academy is in the background on the right. *Photo by Thomas. C. Black, ca. 1913. Carnegie Branch Library for Local History, Boulder Historical Society Collection.*

Today the Chautauqua Auditorium has been restored and is still in use for concerts, programs, and movies. *Photo by author, 1993.*

As part of the fiftieth anniversary celebration of the discovery of silver at Caribou, the Boulder County Metal Mining Association held a rock drilling contest in Chautauqua Park. Miners were timed as they drilled by hand into a large granite rock. Other contests included the "handsomest baby," "the ugliest man," and a prize to the mother from the mountains having the largest family present. *Photo by Ed Tangen, 1919. Carnegie Branch Library for Local History, Boulder Historical Society Collection.*

Here fashionably dressed women look back at Chautauqua Auditorium. Perhaps the woman on the right is taking a photograph with her Kodak. The invention of paper film made these handheld cameras popular with tourists in the first decade of the twentieth century. Photo ca. 1906. *Carnegie Branch Library for Local History, Boulder Historical Society Daily Camera Collection.*

The Dining Hall was initially built to serve the Chautauqua summer residents who lived, but couldn't cook, in tents. After permanent cottages were built, however, many guests still preferred the Dining Hall. After good plain food and delicious pies were consumed, the floor was cleared for dancing. *Photo by Joseph Bevier Sturtevant, ca. 1910. Carnegie Branch Library for Local History, Boulder Historical Society Collection.*

The Dining Hall still serves meals today. As in the early days, visitors enjoy sitting on the balcony and looking north over Boulder. *Photo by author, 2005.*

Chautauqua Mesa Ski Area, complete with rope tow, began in the winter of 1947–1948. Cost per day was $1.00 for adults and 50¢ for children. It operated intermittently until 1962. Photo ca. 1950s. *Carnegie Branch Library for Local History, Boulder Historical Society Daily Camera Collection.*

CHAPTER TEN

SOUTH BOULDER
POSTWAR GROWTH

In 1864, the same year as the Sand Creek Massacre, James B. Viele and his son Jefferson left Illinois for Colorado Territory. Their three yoke of oxen and one yoke of cows pulled a 10-horsepower threshing machine, the first to reach Boulder.

Viele homesteaded south of Boulder but spent most of those first years taking his thresher from farm to farm to harvest wheat, barley, and oats. Five horses were hitched to each of two strong beams radiating from a vertical shaft. As the horses walked around and around in a circle, the shaft turned the mechanism of the grain separator.

In 1878, Viele replaced the horsepower model with a new steam-threshing machine. This was one of the first of its kind in the Boulder area, and again he was in demand. He and his sons slept out in the fields and were fed by the farmers' wives and daughters.

Another homesteader in the South Boulder area was William "Billy" Martin. With his wife, Ida, this ex-prospector turned his wealth from the Caribou mine into productive farmland. Timothy hay was his main crop. He also raised cattle, chickens, and horses.

Between 1886 and 1932, several railroads ran their trains over the tracks on what now is South Broadway. A small station at Park Avenue (Baseline Road) served the area south of town, which remained a quiet farming community for many years. Billy Martin died in 1925. Until her death in 1942, Ida Martin remained on the farm in what became known as Martin Acres.

By 1955, Boulder was a city of nearly thirty thousand people. South Boulder was beginning to be developed, largely because of the relocation of the National Bureau of Standards (now the National Institute of Standards and Technology) from Washington, D.C. Residents of Boulder donated a wide open field for its site. The Rocky Flats Atomic Energy Project, 9 miles south of Boulder, had recently been completed and employed one thousand people. The philosophy of the time was that cities didn't just happen; they had to be built by corporations. World War II was over, and Boulder was caught up in a period of vigorous growth.

Longtime Boulder resident Vergyl Reynolds began planning the Martin Acres Subdivision and the Table Mesa Shopping Center in the mid1950s. Meanwhile, Basemar Shopping Center was opened in 1956. The completion of the first part of the Table Mesa Shopping Center in 1961 coincided with the building of treeless tracts of new homes in the surrounding area. In 1964, construction was begun on the laboratory and office building of the National Center for Atmospheric Research.

With the rapid growth in the Table Mesa area in the 1960s and 1970s, South Boulder as well as the rest of the city developed a concern for open space. As NCAR was being built, the city of Boulder debated about and then purchased the land south of Chautauqua and in front of the Flatirons called Enchanted Mesa. In 1976, Boulder voters approved the Danish plan restricting the number of building permits issued by the city. Viele Lake, next to the South Boulder Recreation Center, and the Martin Acres Subdivision have retained, in name only, a portion of South Boulder's prewar past.

When Green Mountain Cemetery was established in 1904, it was out in the country. Columbia (Pioneer) Cemetery had become run-down. As soon as the new facility opened, family members transferred ninety-one bodies to the new facility. Broadway (now 20th Street) ended at its gates. Photo ca. 1908. *Carnegie Branch Library for Local History, Boulder Historical Society Daily Camera Collection.*

The house (but not the old gate) is still standing on the southwest corner of 20th Street and King Avenue. The cemetery honored its commitment to the families of the re-interred as well as others who chose it for its perpetual care. A. A. Brookfield, a fifty-niner, was one of the Boulder pioneers buried in Columbia Cemetery who was moved to Green Mountain Cemetery. *Photo by author, 2005.*

President Dwight David Eisenhower visited Boulder on September 14, 1954, to dedicate the opening of the National Bureau of Standards. Schools were dismissed so the children could see him. Eisenhower promised Boulderites a richer and better life. He was the only president to visit Boulder while in office. *Photo by James H. Roberts, 1954. Carnegie Branch Library for Local History, Boulder Historical Society Daily Camera Collection.*

In 1949, the National Bureau of Standards chose a 200-acre site for its buildings. The site was on a two-lane road out of the city. Photo 1949. *Carnegie Branch Library for Local History, Boulder Historical Society Daily Camera Collection.*

The former National Bureau of Standards has been renamed the National Institute of Standards and Technology. Boulder's federal laboratories also include the National Oceanic and Atmospheric Administration as well as the National Telecommunications and Information Administration. Research ranges from climate prediction to atomic timekeeping. *Photo by author, 2005.*

The National Bureau of Standards relocated twelve hundred people to Boulder. All needed a place to live and shop. In 1956, Basemar Shopping Center opened, with Busley's Super Market as its anchor store. Photo 1956. *Carnegie Branch Library for Local History, Boulder Historical Society Daily Camera Collection.*

Although Basemar Shopping Center has gone through several changes, the basic configuration is the same. *Photo by author, 2005.*

The original buildings of Table Mesa Village Shopping Center were under construction when this photo of South Boulder was taken. Its anchor store was Joyce's Supermarket. The adjoining subdivisions were too new to have trees. Photo 1961. *Carnegie Branch Library for Local History, Boulder Historical Society Daily Camera Collection.*

With money from his silver mine in Caribou, William "Billy" Martin homesteaded Hayslope Farm, ca. 1876. The house is still standing at 15 South 35th Street, but the surrounding farmlands have given way to the Martin Acres subdivision. *Photo by author, 2005.*

As the city moved south, Boulder needed a second high school. In 1961, Fairview High School opened in the building known today as Nevin Platt Middle School, near Baseline Reservoir. Then, in 1971, the current Fairview High School opened on Greenbriar Boulevard. Here, in 1973, the Fairview Band posed on its athletic field. *Carnegie Branch Library for Local History, Boulder Historical Society collection.*

Twenty years later, the surroundings looked essentially the same. The school added an east wing, housing physical education and instrumental music facilities. *Photo by author, 1993.*

The turnpike to Denver opened in 1952. Until 1967, cars had to stop under the bridge at Broomfield and pay a toll. It cost 15¢ to go to Broomfield and 25¢ to get to Federal Boulevard. This view looks south from the bridge joining Table Mesa Drive and South Boulder Road. Photo 1952. *Carnegie Branch Library for Local History, Boulder Historical Society Daily Camera Collection.*

U.S. Highway 36 is no longer a toll road. Many commuters who use it work in Boulder and have found more afford-able housing in Lafayette and Louisville. Today the 47th Street Bypass, crossing the highway in the background, has absorbed much of Boulder's increasing traffic. *Photo by author, 1993.*

CHAPTER ELEVEN

END OF AN ERA
THE CITY MATURES

Boulder is growing and changing every day. In the early years, Boulder struggled for an economic base, demanded the university and the railroads, developed a culture, and entered confidently into the twentieth century. In 1909, the surviving original fifty-niners were honored at Boulder's semicentennial celebration. When they first came across the plains, they never imagined the changes they would witness in a half-century of life in Boulder. New public and commercial buildings, churches, and residences reflected a feeling of pride and permanence.

As a young city, Boulder was almost giddy. It called itself the Athens of the West and the Place to Be. Eben G. Fine traveled all over the country trying to lure people to visit Boulder and the glaciers. Motorists in the 1920s camped for free in city-run auto parks, and trains still came and left every hour.

The Great Depression was sobering, but in Boulder the people created, and supported, the annual Pow Wow Days to lift their spirits. They bravely looked ahead and favored the Art Deco style of architecture when replacing the burned-out Victorian-style Boulder County Court House. The city wasn't old enough to have developed a feel, or a need, for historic preservation.

After World War II, South Boulder exploded with new growth. Soon Boulder itself spread out to the north and east as well. The downtown business district deteriorated. Trains got so little use that the tracks were removed. The postwar housewife drove her car to shopping centers.

Boulder matured in the 1960s. At that time, the people of Boulder talked about revitalizing downtown, buying open space, and limiting growth. An appreciation for the past had taken a century.

In the early 1970s, Historic Boulder, Inc. was formed to recognize and preserve Boulder's historic buildings. The Pearl Street pedestrian mall revitalized the downtown business district. Business owners removed the metal siding that had covered up their storefronts. Pride and interest in Boulder came back in style.

Today, Boulder's problems are by no means solved. Indeed, the city's biggest challenges, which include transportation, the economy, housing, and the environment, still lie ahead. A look at the past gives perspective to the future. It is to be hoped that Boulder residents will address their problems as a mature city instead of as merely the Place to Be.

In 1957, the last of Boulder's depots was built by the Colorado & Southern Railroad. It was west of the tracks and north of the wye between Pearl Street and Valmont Road. Photo 1957. *Carnegie Branch Library for Local History, Boulder Historical Society Daily Camera Collection.*

Union Pacific and Colorado & Southern tracks crossed at the wye north of Pearl Street and east of 30th Street. Photo ca. 1957. *Carnegie Branch Library for Local History, Boulder Historical Society Daily Camera Collection.*

Passenger service was discontinued in 1967, and the Union Pacific tracks were removed. In 1981, the Colorado & Southern was merged into the Burlington Northern Railroad. The last depot was discontinued in 1985, although freight trains come through daily. Today the depot is a shop and storage for Sutherlands Lumber. The building's flat roof is barely visible behind the freight cars. *Photo by author, 1993.*

FOR FURTHER READING

Barker, Jane Valentine. *Historic Homes of Boulder, Colorado.* Boulder: Pruett, 1979.

———. *76 Historic Homes of Boulder, Colorado.* Boulder: Pruett, 1976.

Bixby, Amos. "History of Boulder County," in *History of Clear Creek and Boulder Valleys.* Chicago: O. L. Baskin, 1880.

Cobb, Harrison S. *Prospecting Our Past.* Longmont: Book Lode, 1999.

Crossen, Forest. *The Switzerland Trail of America.* Boulder: Pruett, 1962.

Davis, William E. *Glory Colorado, A History of the University of Colorado 1858–1963.* Boulder: Pruett, 1965.

Deno, William R. *Body & Soul, Architectural Style at the University of Colorado at Boulder.* Boulder: University of Colorado, 1994.

Dyni, Anne Quinby. *Back to the Basics: The Frontier Schools of Boulder County, Colorado 1860–1960.* Boulder: Book Lode, 1991.

Fine, Eben G. *Remembered Yesterdays.* Boulder: Johnson, 1957.

Galey, Mary. *The Grand Assembly: The Story of Life at the Colorado Chautauqua.* Boulder: First Flatiron Press, 1981.

Gladden, Sanford. *Boulder Firsts: A Source-book of Beginnings in Boulder, Colorado.* Boulder: Boulder Genealogical Society, 1972.

———. *Hotels of Boulder, Colorado, from 1860.* Boulder: Johnson, 1970.

———. *Improvements in Boulder.* Boulder: Boulder Genealogical Society, 1984.

———. *The Early Days of Boulder, Colorado,* Vols. 1 & 2. Boulder: Boulder Genealogical Society, 1983.

Jones, William C., and Noel T. Holley. *The Kite Route, Story of the Denver & Interurban Railroad.* Boulder: Pruett, 1986.

Meier, Thomas J. *Ed Tangen, The Pictureman.* Boulder: Boulder Creek Press, 1994.

Ormes, Robert M. *Railroads and the Rockies, A Record of the Lines in and Near Colorado.* Denver: Sage Books, 1963.

———. *Tracking Ghost Railroads in Colorado.* Colorado Springs: Century One Press, 1975.

Pettem, Silvia. *Behind the Badge: 125 Years of the Boulder, Colorado, Police Department.* Ward: Book Lode, 2003.

———. *Boulder: A Sense of Time and Place.* Longmont: Book Lode, 2000.

———. *Chautauqua Centennial, A Hundred Years of Programs.* Longmont: Book Lode, 1998.

———. *Legend of a Landmark: A History of the Hotel Boulderado.* Missoula: Pictorial Histories, 1997.

———. *Separate Lives: The Story of Mary Rippon.* Longmont: Book Lode, 1999.

Repplier, E. O. *As a Town Grows: The Schools of Boulder, Colorado, In the Pageant of the Years 1860–1959.* Boulder: Boulder County School District No. 3, 1959.

Rogers, Maria M. *In Other Words: Oral Histories of the Colorado Frontier.* Golden: Fulcrum Publishing, 1995.

Schoolland, John B. *A Pioneer Church.* Boulder: Johnson, 1972.

———. *Boulder in Perspective.* Boulder: Johnson, 1980.

———. *Boulder Then and Now.* Boulder: Pruett, 1967.

Sewall, Jane. *Jane, Dear Child.* Boulder: University of Colorado Press, 1957.

Smith, Phyllis. A *Look at Boulder: From Settlement to City.* Boulder: Pruett, 1981.

INDEX